TRAINING FOR SCALPER

Performing quick operations
on the stock exchange

Lerbius Mark

Warren Stormer Publishing Company

Copyright © 2021 Lerbius Mark

All rights reserved

The characters and events portrayed in this book are fictitious. Any similarity to real persons, living or dead, is coincidental and not intended by the author.

No part of this book may be reproduced, or stored in a retrieval system, or transmitted in any form or by any means, electronic, mechanical, photocopying, recording, or otherwise, without express written permission of the publisher.

ISBN-13: 9798738879821
ISBN-10: 1477123456

Cover design by: Art Painter
Library of Congress Control Number: 2018675309
Printed in the United States of America

The market goes up stairs and down the elevator.

DESCRIPTION

The book Training for Scalper is indicated for those operators who already have knowledge of the financial market and have already had a first contact with graphic analysis, although superficial.

Scalper is the speculator who opens operations and closes them quickly, picking up his profit in defined market movements.

Accurate techniques are taught, use of time graphics, always with illustrations of real candles, so you know where to position your order, your stop loss and your stop gain.

It is a fundamental guide for those who want to be a Scalper Trader!

WHAT IS SCALPING?

Scalping is the art of performing short operations, with predefined target, where you enter and exit operations quickly.

The market needs to be volatile, whether up or down. It needs to be a moment of euphoria or a moment of fear. It's easier to operate. It is only in those moments that the scalper acts.

You will position stop loss and stop gain (also known as TP or "Take Profit") so that you protect your raw material (capital) and ensure that you will not return the profit to the market if the quote comes back and you do not pick up your gain.

It is a surgical process. You're not going to open an operation simply by opening. There is a multigraphic technical analysis to be performed so that it is not a complete casino.

Of course, I cannot help but say that the market is rather partly a casino. After all, if it wasn't, it would be a factory of raising millionaires. There would already be robots scattered all over the world performing the best operations and taking their money.

Technical analysis exists to reduce this "roulette". The idea is for you to go into operations that have a 70% or more chance of working. That is the play you should keep in mind.

Entering an operation with a 30% chance of success is what you do not want to do, and you are never going to do it. Or never again.

CAN ANYONE BE SCALPER?

A Scalper needs to have a lot of discipline.

You need to be a strategist, you really want to manage your operations, and you need to be emotional for that.

If you do not like to position stop loss, if you do not like to position stop gain, do not want to keep following the price of the asset carefully after entering the operation, then you do not have profile to be a scalper.

The scalper is the candle brusher. You need to evaluate the chart and some of the flow so that your operations have the assertiveness necessary to seek the long-dreamed consistency.

Such an operator does not even need to read newspapers. You just need to know about events that can generate extreme volatility and wait for them to happen to operate.

In short, the scalper, although he does few operations on the day, needs to stay focused on the chart because often opportunities will arise throughout the day, and you may end up not taking advantage of them if you are not attentive.

In addition, you need to be available to trade at times of more market volatility, which are in the first hour of trading and in the last hour of trading. These moments are essential. At the very least, the scalper needs to be operating on these two occasions.

WHY SCALP?

The answer is simple: To diversify your investments!

Imagine an investor who allocates 100% of his capital in Position.

After a big market swell, their positions will depreciate immensely and the investor will spend months seeing their money eroded, while others will be taking advantage of the fall and making money.

Is it right to do only Scalp? Also, not!

The secret to success is balance, and it is what you should seek.

The capital you allocate in any Day Trade practice is venture capital.

It is that capital that you will use to generate more capital on the basis of speculation.

You are a long-term investor, but like Scalper, you are a speculator.

In addition, you can set up a Swing Trade or Position position, and then operate by scalping related assets, seeking to optimize your earnings on days when your position assets retract ed prices.

RISK CONTROL AND ACCOUNT SEPARATION

The first thing you should do before performing any Day Trade operation is to separate your accounts.

An account will be your Investments (shares that pay dividends, growth companies, etc.).

In another account, preferably at another broker, you will have your venture capital, and preferably with free brokerage.

You will establish your maximum risk e.g., daily, or weekly.

You will for example take $50.00 and allocate in your risk broker, the one you have chosen to scalp. That's the value of your risk. It is the value you will use to operate.

What happens if you mix your reserve capital with day trade capital?

The broker will grant you margin based on that capital, and then you run the huge risk of ending up leveraged in a practice you should not.

> *Do not forget, the broker is a financial institution. She makes money from her need for capital. Do not wash.*

And most importantly, do not operate in the real market before using simulator. It is the easiest way to lose money.

It is like learning to ride bikes without the wheels. You are going to worry all over while you could have trained your balance first.

SET THE VALUE FOR EACH TRADE!

To set the amount of capital you will use in the trades just pick up your capital that you allocated at the broker per month, for example, you have separated $50.00 to scalping at the broker.

Let us say you will trade for only 10 trading sessions in the month, then give the value of $ 5.00 per day for trades.

You have set that you will make 4 trades per day at most. So, your stop loss should be a maximum of $1.25 and so you will have good control of your operations and your money.

Your initial goal will not be to get rich but to try to end the month with your $50.00 or more in the account! That is what you need to have in mind.

You are going to work hard for this. You're going to try harder, of course. You're not going to play for the tie. But you need to know that you're still building your experience. A short step is a good start.

Another primordial thing, you need to have Stop Loss and Stop Gain!

Cannot operate without a defined target (gain). It's throwing money away. You're going to give it all back because you're a Scalper. Quick operations. Take your profit and get out.

EVERYTHING IS EMBEDDED IN THE PRICES.

The first thing a Scalper should know is that the chart already brings all the effect of news and landmark events.

Of course, apart from catastrophes that are called "tail events", that is, a large explosion in the White House, airplanes hitting buildings etc.

Even in these cases, scalper is protected by stop loss, and then you will see the market going backwards a lot and quickly. But it has already come out of the operation, while long-term investors and even swing trade investors will suffer more.

The coronavirus pandemic may have taken small investors by surprise, but the charts already pointed to an exceedingly high level of buying in February, even with the level of risk at alarming levels around the world.

Institutional investors were already exiting the assets. Warren Buffet, for example, had already undone his positions on airlines.

Anyway, you as scalper do not have to worry about any of this. Just with your chart.

TREND

The Scalper should always be aware of the trend of the asset that will operate.

Under no circumstances should you operate against the trend. It is unprofitable and extremely dangerous.

It is like swimming against the tide. You will be able to move forward, but if you were to swim in favor, you would be more successful in your work.

When I say dangerous, I do not say that an operation will be dangerous, but rather the sequence of operations you are going to do is that they are dangerous, because you are going to end up making more mistakes than you are getting.

A wrong operation gives you a Stop Loss. But if you insist, there may be 3 or 4 stops there and that is when you should stop operating, following your risk management.

Why stop? Simple. It means you didn't identify the trend correctly. It's like a text that you wrote yourself and reread several times to find an error. You won't find it, you're hooked. So, you better close the book and open it after you rest.

That said, we have that the trend can be HIGH or LOW.

If it is in an uptrend, it is because the market understands that the asset is cheap and can rise.

If you are in a downtrend, the market considers that the asset is expensive, and so it is much more likely that sales will occur than purchases in that asset.

The trend is formed by the big players and the flow of foreign capital that enters the stock exchange, and more precisely in the asset itself.

After all, when the whole world is excited to buy a certain asset, this indicates a much larger volume of movement.

But the trend is also influenced by price memory. This is because if I know that an asset was quoted at $40.00 before a large, generalized fall, and the asset suffered nothing from the reason for the fall, then it quickly creates an uptrend, seeking to reach that price memorized by the market.

That is, supply and demand (buyers with cash and sellers making their profits) and the memory of prices drive the direction, while the institutional (large banks and treasuries) and foreigners (international capital) generate the volume.

Do you always have a tendency? No.

It is possible that at that time there is no defined trend.

> *"When there is no trend, scalper does not act!"*

Next, we will learn to identify the trend of the asset, to prevent us from active in assets without trend, or even worse, against the trend.

IDENTIFYING THE ASSET TREND

The trend is basically characterized by ascending tops and bottoms or tops and descending bottoms.

Let us see:

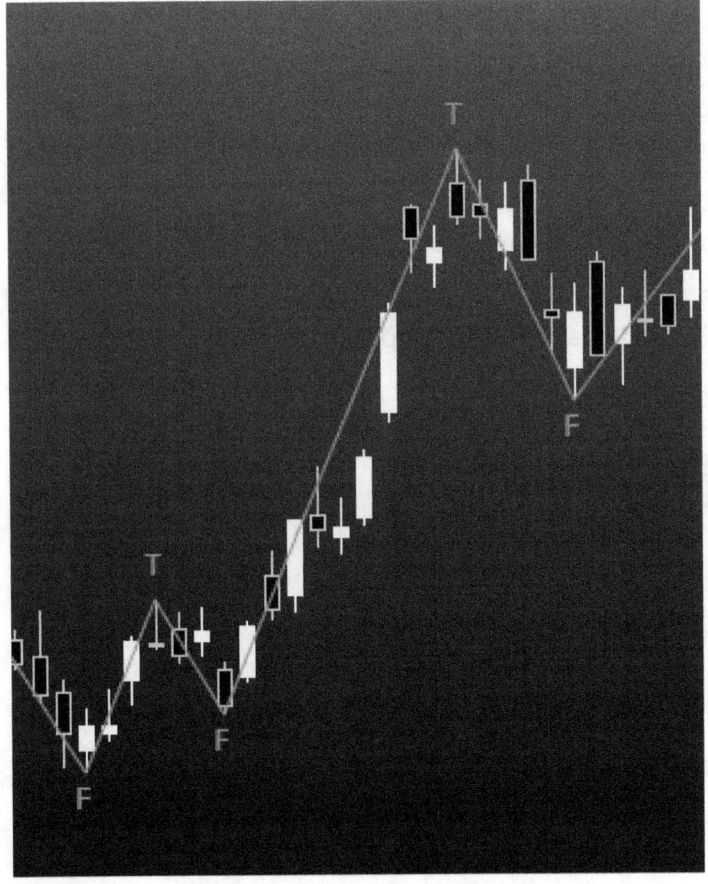

Notice that the asset has been making higher bottoms and tops.

The top letter T and the bottom letter F.

That is, the bottom is always higher than the previous bottom and the top is always higher than the previous top.

In the above case, we have an uptrend.

> *"The trend lasts until it is replaced."*

Of course, this will not last forever.

We must be vigilant to identify when such a trend can change, so as not to enter a Scalp at the end of a trend.

It is much better to enter at the beginning of a trend. The chance of a hit is extremely high.

But how do I define Tops and Bottoms? How do I find them?

I suggest using detector indicators from tops and bottoms. They are automated and prevent you from having the visual work of finding the tops.

Every indicator of this has the configuration of how many periods you want to characterize a top or a bottom.

That is, there are how many candles will need to go for the bottom to be deep, and for the top to be top.

You should make this adjustment by changing the number of periods and looking at your chart to identify what best approximates the behavior of the asset.

TREND CONFIRMATION

Trend confirmation is simple.

If it is an uptrend, this trend will be confirmed when the last top breakout occurs.

If the price passes above that level, the maintenance of the uptrend is confirmed.

In this case the last top is called pivot, and the breakout of this pivot will confirm the continuation of the trend.

> The downtrend is only confirmed when the previous fundist breakout occurs, and the upright trend is only confirmed when the previous top breakout occurs.

In the situation of being in a downtrend, the trend will be confirmed if there is a breakout of the last fund, that is, the price of the asset should fall below the last fund recorded on the chart.

Trend confirmation is important because if you are not in the operation it is your chance to open it.

And if you are already in the operation, it is the time when you must move your stop to the last top or bottom, thereby ensuring your profit.

After all, if you make a lower bottom in the uptrend, the alert is on and you as Scalper does not cross yellow signal. You only go green.

TREND CHANGE

While the asset is making tops and bottoms up, great. Uptrend.

We can guarantee you are on an uptrend.

Or if you are making ascends and bottoms down, fine. Downtrend.

But at any given point, it is possible that in the uptrend it will make a lower bottom than the previous one, or that it makes a lower top than the previous one.

And in the downtrend, it is possible that the next fund will end up being larger than the previous one or that the next top is larger than the previous one, mischaracterizing the trend.

That is, the asset failed to maintain the trend. At this point we must stop and pay attention. We can't operate until we identify the next move.

TRAINING FOR SCALPER

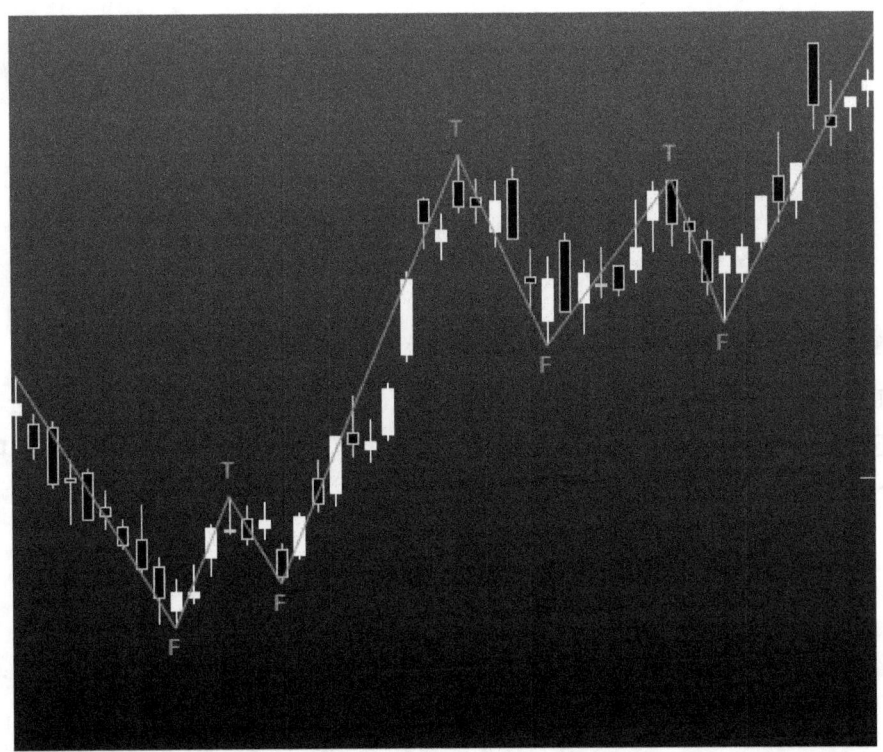

Notice that the third top is below the second top, generating an alert signal on the Scalper.

At this point, you should wait to see if the previous background will also be "lost".

If so, the asset has lost the uptrend and possibly reversed dramatically.

But it is also possible that it makes a higher background as in the figure above. In this case, the Scalper must wait to see if the last top will be "broken", that is, if it will make a top above it.

As we see, the alarm was false, and the uptrend remained strong.

SECONDARY TREND

The secondary trend is the short-term trend.

In the short term, that is, in smaller chart time, there is a top larger than another and a fund larger than the other, but in the larger chart, that is, in the primary trend, it is only a mere correction.

In number 1 we have a graph with time 15 minutes and 2 we have a graph of 5 minutes.

The main scalper analysis should always be done in the larger time screen.

If you operate only the 5-minute chart you will end up selling thinking it was a trend change, when in fact it was just a retraction on the 15-minute chart.

So, the ideal is to operate always looking at two-time graphics, one being larger to be your guide during the day and the other to define the point of entry into operations.

MOMENT TO ACT.

Scalper will act in two main moments.

The first is in the test of the last top (or bottom if it is downtrend). You can operate both the breakout and the trend reversal (if it does not break and reverse the trend).

The other moment is in the correction, that is, in the retraction that the asset gives (generating a new higher bottom) and preparing for the ascent. Or in the case of the downtrend when it generates a new lower top and then following the descent according to the trend.

We will see that the tops can be graphic tops, tops of a congestion channel, top of a flag, as well as the bottoms.

In any case, the scalper will always try to identify the attention candle and the return candle.

It is these candles that will allow the scalper to activate your attention at the maximum level and prepare to open your position, whether bought or sold.

BREAKOUT OF THE LAST TOP OR BOTTOM (PIVOT)

Let us look at the first moment, which is the breakup of the last top (in the case of the uptrend)

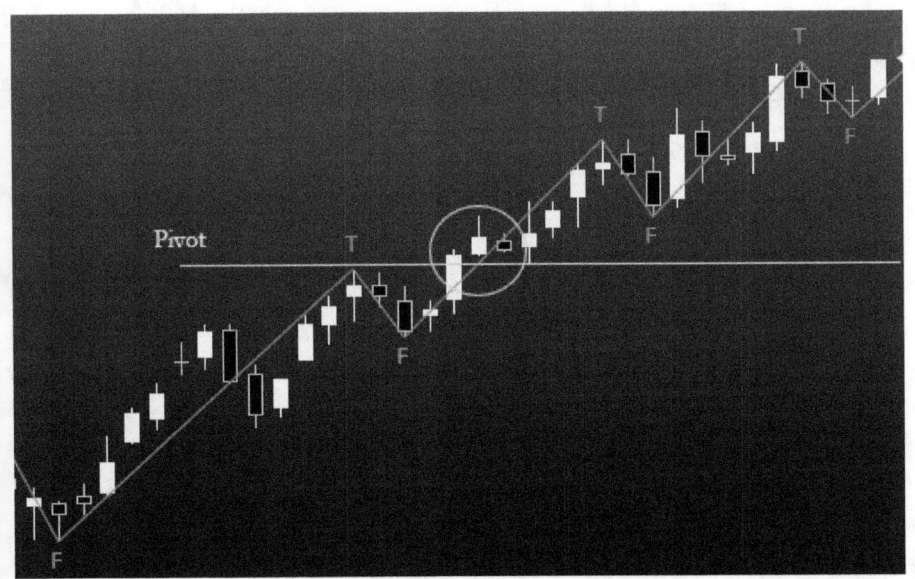

In the image we can see where the PIVOT point is.

In the uptrend, the pivot is formed at the time the last top is confirmed.

And the last top is confirmed when you form the next bottom!

In this case, you can operate the breakout from the last top, as long as the bottom has been higher than the previous one, i.e., full uptrend.

In this case, it is very safe to enter the operation purchased there at the exact moment the price breaks the last top, that is, in the circled area.

This moment is called "euphoria." The market usually breaks the last top with high volume and large sail.

Your Stop-Loss will be just below the last fund, because if the next fund is not higher than this, there is danger of trend reversal, then you exit the operation!

CORRECTION OR RETRACTION

Another great time when scalper initiates the operation is when a retraction occurs.

The retraction is nothing more than the "breath" of the market.

This breath always exists, because speculators who have already made a profit from the rise will sell to secure the money in their pockets. Usually, partial sales.

In retractions the volume is always lower than in euphoria, and this is an analysis criterion to be followed by scalper.

See in The Picture:

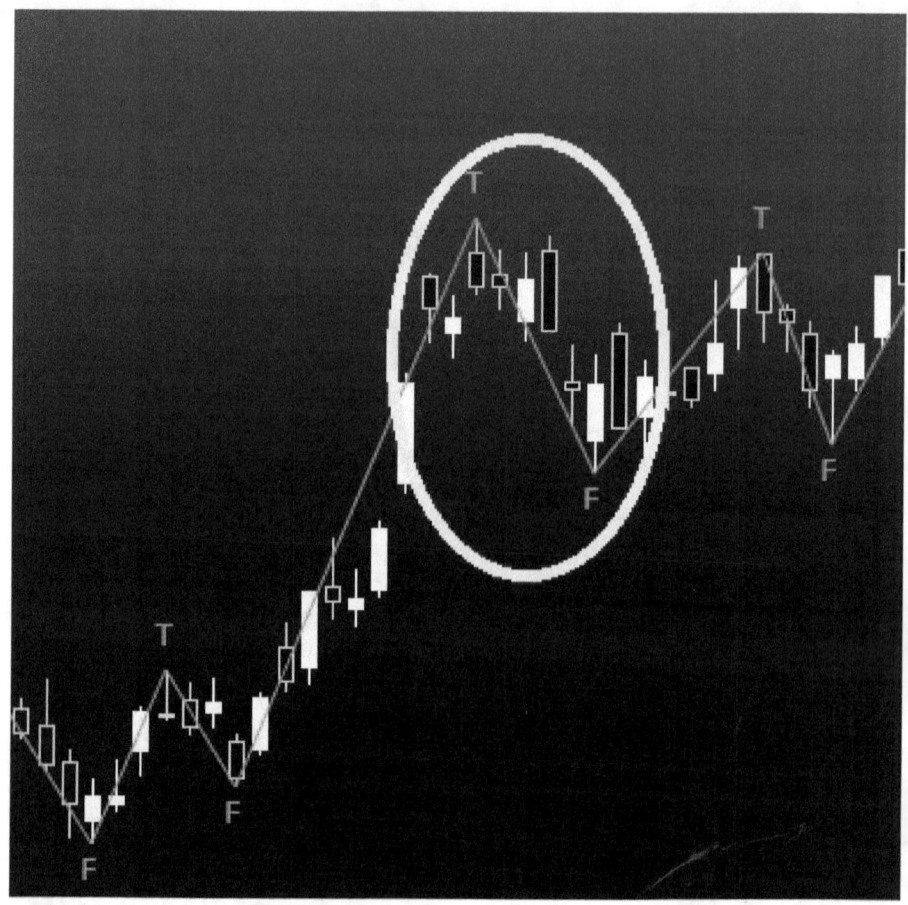

That is the moment of retraction circled in yellow.

It is the breath of the market before following its definite trend.

Scalper will try to buy there at the bottom, at the end of the rest, the breath, the retraction, to catch the next wave high.

A common target is the next top. That's because usually the market will test the previous top. So even if it does not get over the top, at least you have made your profit, even if it is in partial form.

REALIZATION X FEAR

It is important for Scalper to be aware of breaking news and market indicators such as employment index, payroll, oil stocks, etc.

This is because the retractions, that is, the small price corrections, are usually generated only by achievements or shortage of buyers (at high) or sellers (downtown).

When there is fear, the market usually acts more abruptly, more aggressively.

Fear shakes the emotional, it shocks the entire market.

If the current us stocked oil contingent is close to being announced, you will not operate oil companies at that time. You are going to wait.

Because there can be a sudden reversal of the trend because of fear or euphoria.

Scalper does not want to be clear. Scalper acts with a defined tendency. In peace.

VOLUME INDICATOR

Whenever you are analyzing the input in an operation, the volume should be considered in your chart.

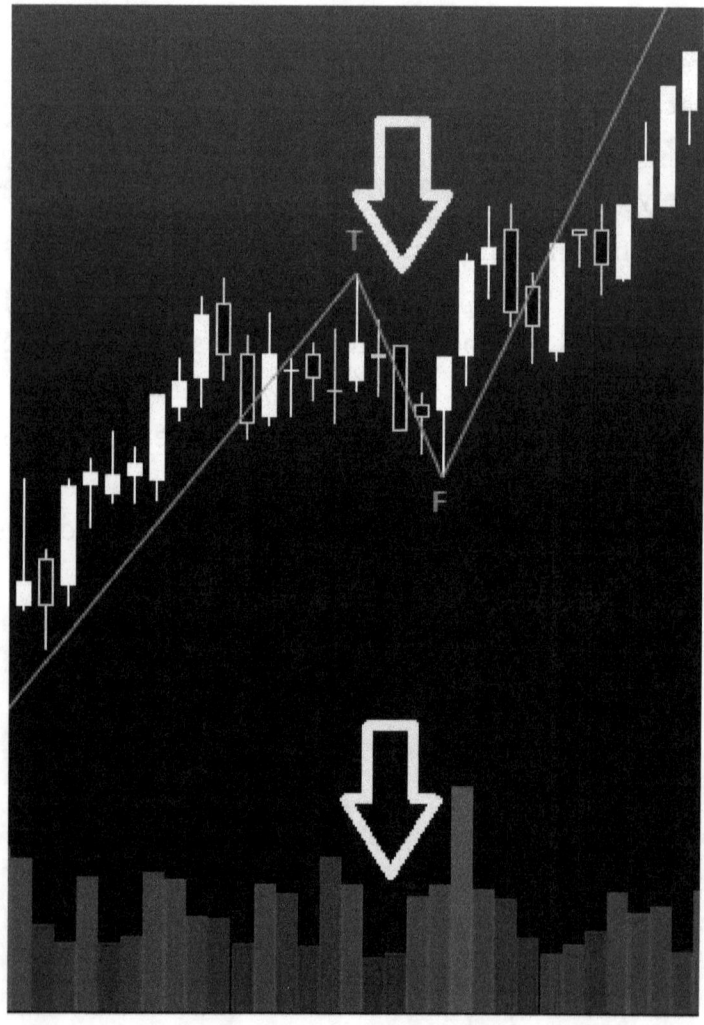

As already mentioned, in the retractions the volume is reduced in relation to euphoria.

In the yellow arrows we see the retraction and its volume, much lower than the ascent candles of the asset, characterizing its uptrend.

Scalper can enter more quietly in this operation; it is an indicator of more assertiveness for your trade. Of course, always positioning the Stop Loss.

What if that "retraction" was large, higher than average?

In this case, there is no opening to perform the scalp, and one should look for another asset or wait for a more appropriate signal, such as the disruption of the last top.

After all if there is volume of fall there is fear. Difficult to maintain an uptrend with this setting.

PRICE RETURN POINT

One of the most important topics for Scalper is precisely to observe where the return of prices may be. That is, a place where there is a reasonable probability of reversal.

When there is a return point, scalper should wait for confirmation of the trend change.

We say above that a downtrend occurs when there are bottoms and bottoms down, i.e., the current top is lower than the previous top and the current bottom is lower than the previous bottom.

However, at the moment this is broken by one side, that is, does not make a lower bottom, we have a Return Point.

Either the asset will keep falling or it reverts to rise. And at that moment the operation of scalper is possible to purchase the asset. The operation will be up because the asset has weakened its power of fall.

This is great for scalper, as the Stop will be short, just below the previous bottom. Yes, below the bottom. After all, remember that if you break the previous fund on a downtrend, the trend is confirmed!

Okay, but is it any number of candles that allow me to determine that there is a turning point?

No. The correct is at least 3 previous candles making bottoms and descending tops so that you characterize that the 4th candle, if not bottom below the 3rd candle, is a return point.

TRAINING FOR SCALPER

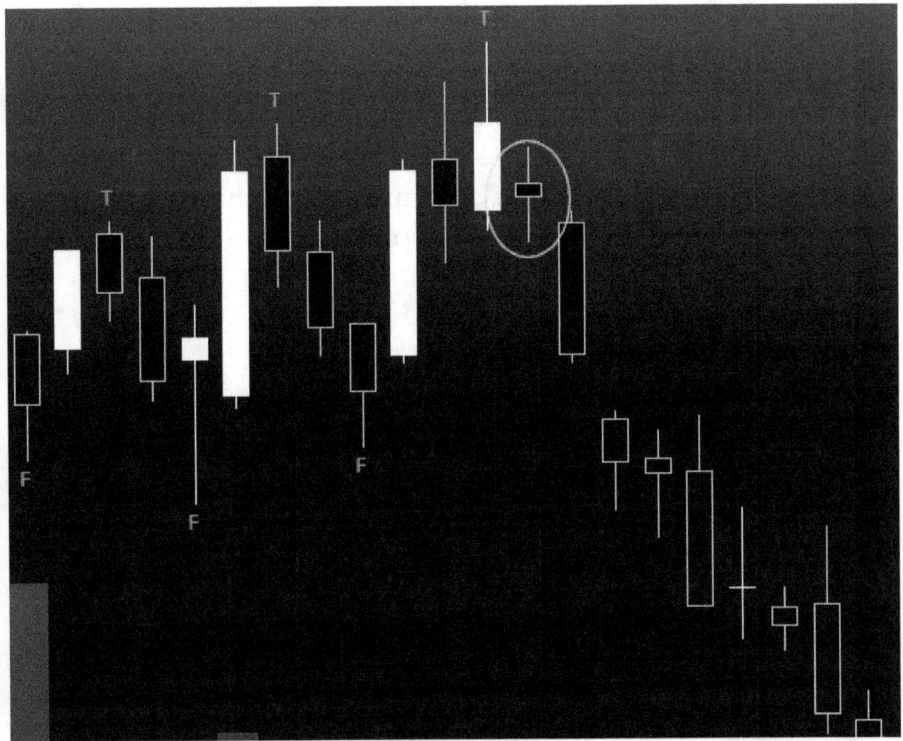

Notice the image that the return candle is circled in yellow. In it we see the break of the sequence of tops and ascending bottoms. The entry into the operation will be exactly when the last bottom, that is, the bottom of the circled candle, is lost.

There will be confirmed the reversal of the trend.

If the next candle cannot make a top above the circled candle, which is the return point, at least the market will be consolidated (no trend). That is why your stop loss is there at the maximum of the circled candle.

In the picture we see that the return has been confirmed.

Most likely you focus only on the circulated candle and will ignore the other candles. But if you look closely, see the second bottom from left to right.

The next candle reversed so fast that there was no time to enter the operation. The huge high sail (called marobozu). She was my return point, but I "lost" because the sail was too big. Hey, what's up? How would I get into the operation?

Simple. You're a Scalper. It should change to the smaller chart, as this is where you fine-tune your operation. There surely you would have identified a point of return within this operation and would have succeeded by the size of the candle that formed on the larger chart!

ALERT POINT BEFORE RETURN POINT

There are situations in which scalper should already be attentive and paralyze its actions immediately to wait for the market to progress.

Let us see below an interesting price movement in a defined trend that may be ending.

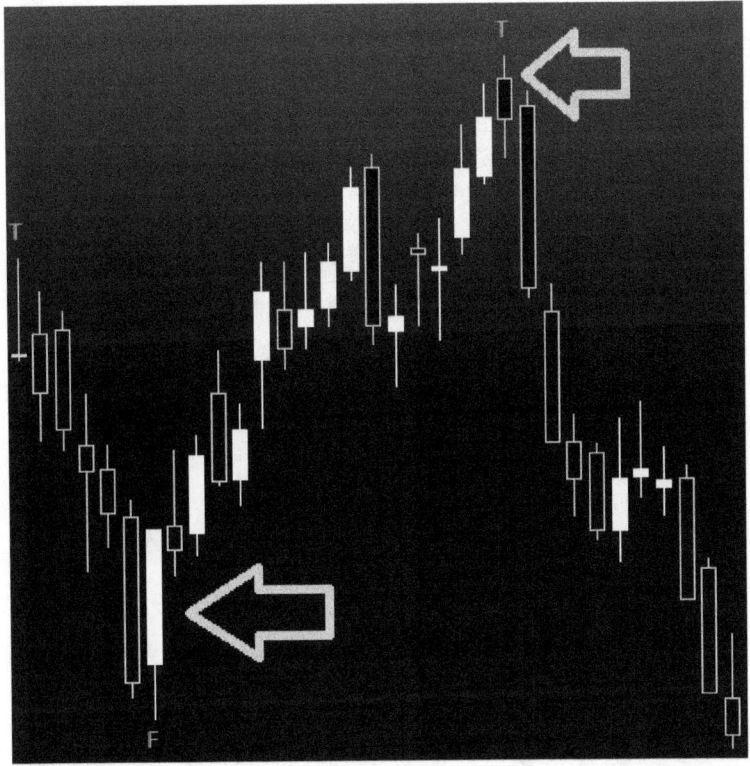

What is in the candles indicated on the arrows?

Notice, the first is a high candle at the end of a low sequence, and the second is a low candle in a high sequence.

These candles are warning points. They're not return points! It is not any positive candle that will reverse an uptrend, and vice versa.

But notice that even the candle pointed at the arrow after downtrend still makes tops and bottoms descending. It's not a turning point. It is a point of attention.

If you go to the shorter time chart, you will see that at that point the asset has already reversed! It is already making bigger tops and bottoms there.

The next candle will possibly be the return point. Unless you reduce the time to time and already do the operation after evaluating that in the shortest time, there was the return.

LATERALIZATION

Lateralization occurs when the asset cannot break through the anterior bottom or the previous top.

The candles are oscillating there between the top and the previous bottom, unable to form new extremes.

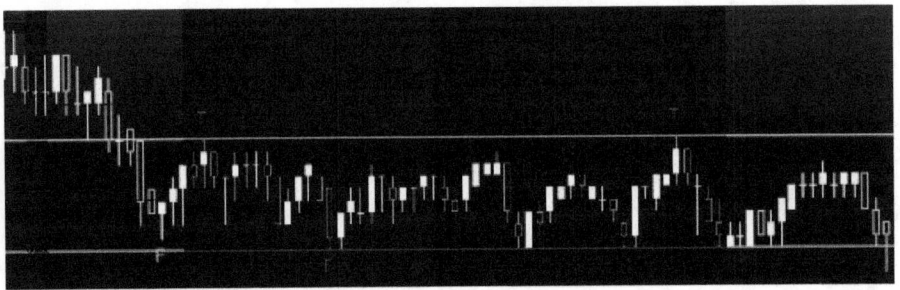

We have in the image the lateralization of the asset since it cannot break the top and the bottom.

Be careful with this "breakup" because the simple fact of passing $0.01 above or below during the formation of the candle does not indicate that there was a breakup. It is necessary to wait for the candle to close. In this case, the longer the time limit, the more assertive the break in the candle closure.

In these cases of lateralization where the top and the previous bottom are not broken, we have the so-called Rectangle which is a graphic figure.

You as scalper can try to buy the bottom of the rectangle by placing stop below the last bottom and sell at the top placing the stop above the last top. But it is not a very assertive operation because sudden movements can lead you to a sequence of stops that can shake your emotional.

In the image above you would succeed, with only 1 stop in more than 80 candles, would give you a nice profit, but it is fair to tell you that not always the garden will be only flowers.

However, imagine that the image above is the longer time picture. If you reduce the time to trade, you will have greatly increased your assertiveness because you can already mark how far the price can go up, and how far it can fall.

From there, in the shorter timechart, you operate searching for return points, while already know their boundaries within the rectangle. (top and bottom of the larger chart)

If the return point to reverse to low is near the top on the larger chart, it is a good place to enter the operation.

There is nothing better when 2 signals at different times coincide. It is the best time to operate.

SUPPORT AND RESISTANCE

We support the point where buyers are considering the price so attractive that they hold the price of falling further.

It is also the time when those who wish to sell short are afraid to open their positions because they suspect that the asset may stop falling at that moment.

In these locations there is the possibility of generating a return point, which will be observed by scalper.

Resistance is the same thing, but on the top side.

It is the place where those bought (those who are positioned in the asset) consider that the asset should not rise anymore and will choose to sell to realize their profits.

Similarly, those who wish to sell short ly plan to open their position there for the same reason.

Return points create supports and resistances. For example, if a stock has been fluctuating for months between $10.00 and $15.00, whenever you get close to $15.00 the volume of purchases will be reduced and possibly whoever bought it will sell because it does not believe it will go up.

The asset will only win that $15.00, that is, this resistance, if some large player mounts a long-term position there, that is, not caring about this resistance, because it believes that the asset is more valuable.

A good example is the case of rectangle lateralization that we saw above. See this scenario again and look at the top row, which is the support, and the bottom row, which is the resistance.

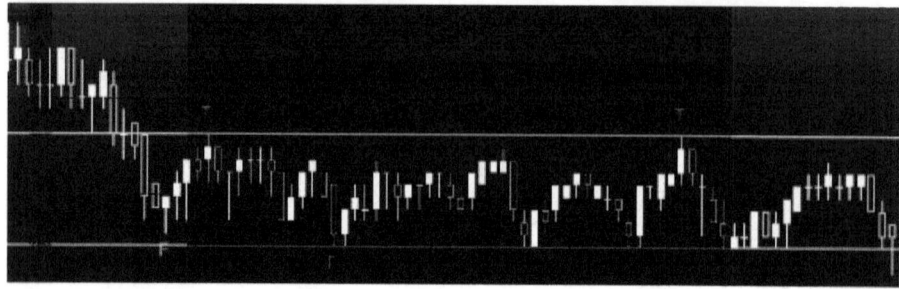

The longer the time, the stronger the support or resistance. This is because the number of negotiations there in price is also higher, forming consensus.

You mark the resistance by connecting the consecutive tops and mark the brackets by connecting the consecutive backgrounds.

These are precisely the ideal points to go into operation because the Stop is truly short.

The more times the price hits the support or resistance and returns, the more reliable this price level is getting.

It is also valid to always mark supports and resistances of the daily chart, because Swing Trade investors use it to trade. They are investors who do not usually follow the prices all day, so usually they will do their analysis at night, to operate the next morning.

The supports and resistances are bipolar. What does that mean?

It means that when the resistance is overcome, after the asset price exceeds it, this resistance automatically becomes a support. Why is that?

Simple. Imagine that at that price level buyers thought it was not valid to buy because the price would possibly return down.

Suddenly, there is a change by some factor and a large volume enters buying the asset, changing that view, and overcoming the support. What's going on? Now there are a huge number of traders who are bought in the asset, that is, who will not sell until they reach their profits.

In addition, investors who were betting that the price would return down (sold short) will have their stops triggered (including you probably) and with that there will be even more buying aggressions to raise prices.

This goes for support equally. It will become a resistance if something happens to the asset and many investors sell their assets or decide to open short positions there for some reason that occurred.

TREND LINES

There is another way to mark supports and resistances, which are through the Uptrend Line and Downtrend Line.

Let us see in the image the tracing of an Uptrend Line:

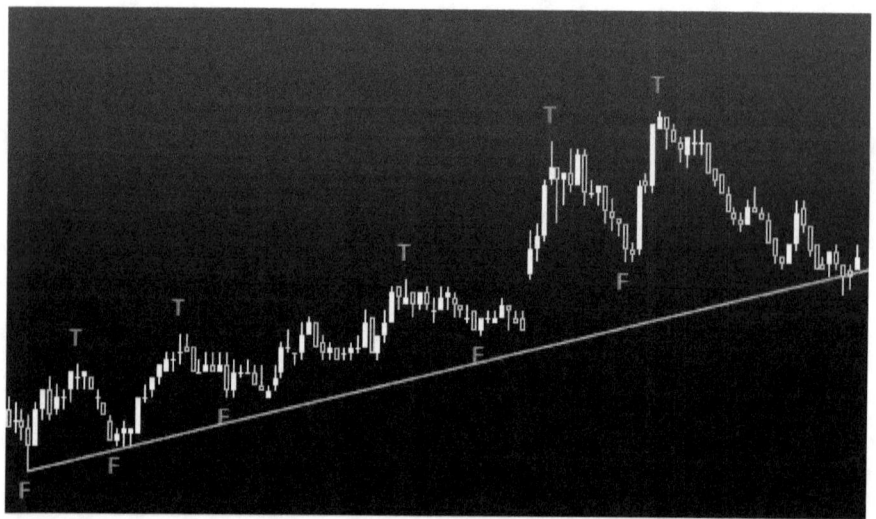

And what is the relevance of Uptrend Line?

Simple. The return points that are there in the vicinity of the Uptrend Line are more valuable because they have greater assertiveness.

The Uptrend Line is the ascent angle of the asset. That's why it works as support. It is the speed of the uptrend of the asset.

Similarly, we have Downtrend Line.

TRAINING FOR SCALPER

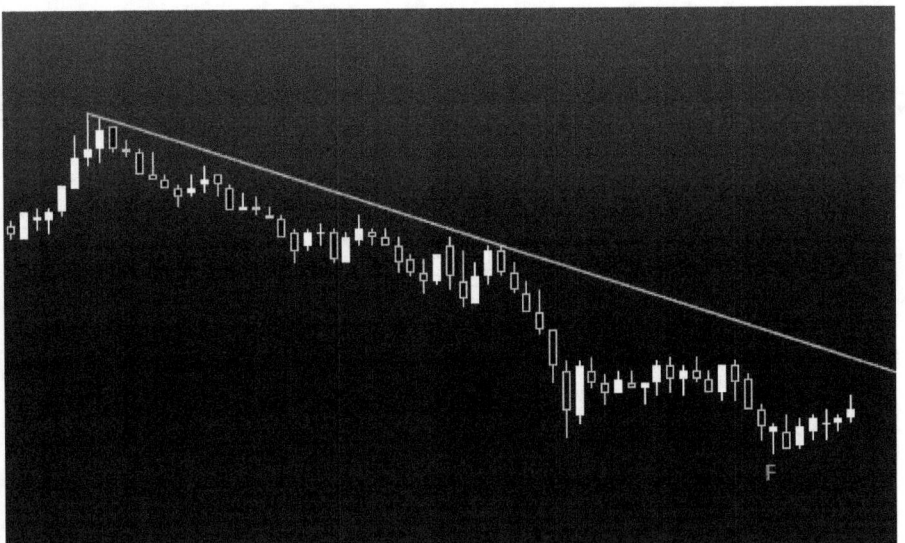

The idea is the same. If you find a return point that is close to Downtrend Line, there is great assertiveness to operate.

And how do I trace the trend line?

Again, it is likely that your platform has such an automatic design. All you have to do is use it by selecting and placing it on the chart.

If not, create a diagonal line by connecting the candles through your wicks as shown in the images.

You need to touch at least 2 points, and the more you play the line.

SECONDARY AND TERTIARY TREND LINE

The primary trendline is the one we drew in the previous topic.

She is the longest-term line. But if we want to be more surgical, we can draw the secondary lines.

To do this, find the second point where the line touches and mark a new line from there, seeking to find another point below, as we see below, where the continuous line is the primary UPTREND LINE, and the dashed line is the secondary UPTREND LINE:

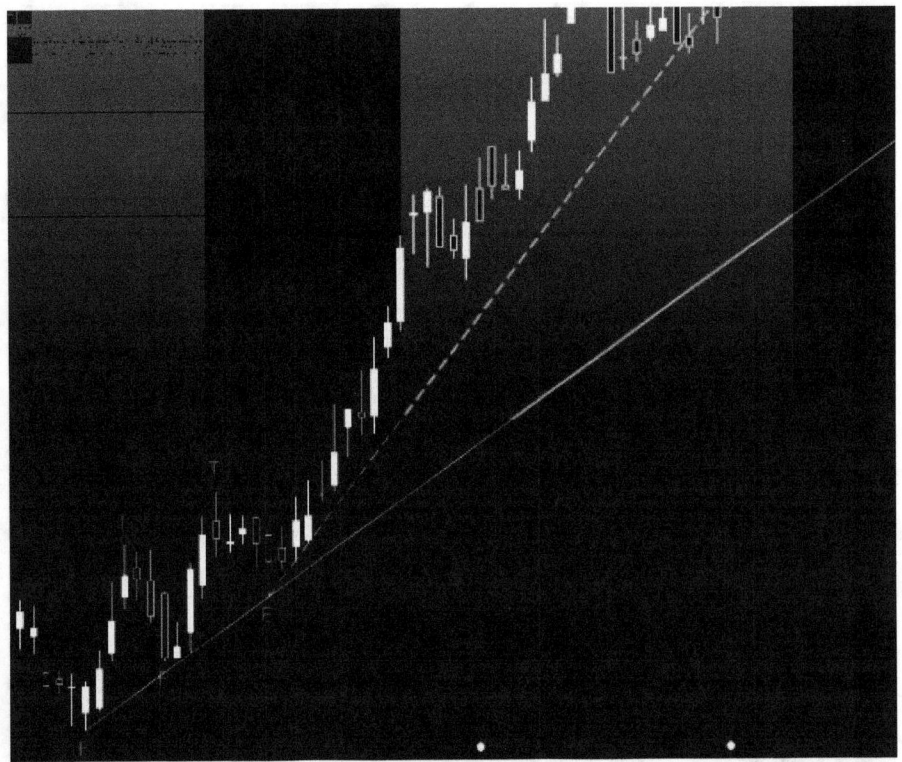

Note that secondary UPTREND LINE has increased the assertiveness of operations because it has picked up a shorter term.

We can move forward and trace the tertiary UPTREND LINE, which will give us the most surgical measure we want to open operations.

Next, the dotted line is the tertiary UPTREND LINE, drawn from the second touch of the secondary line.

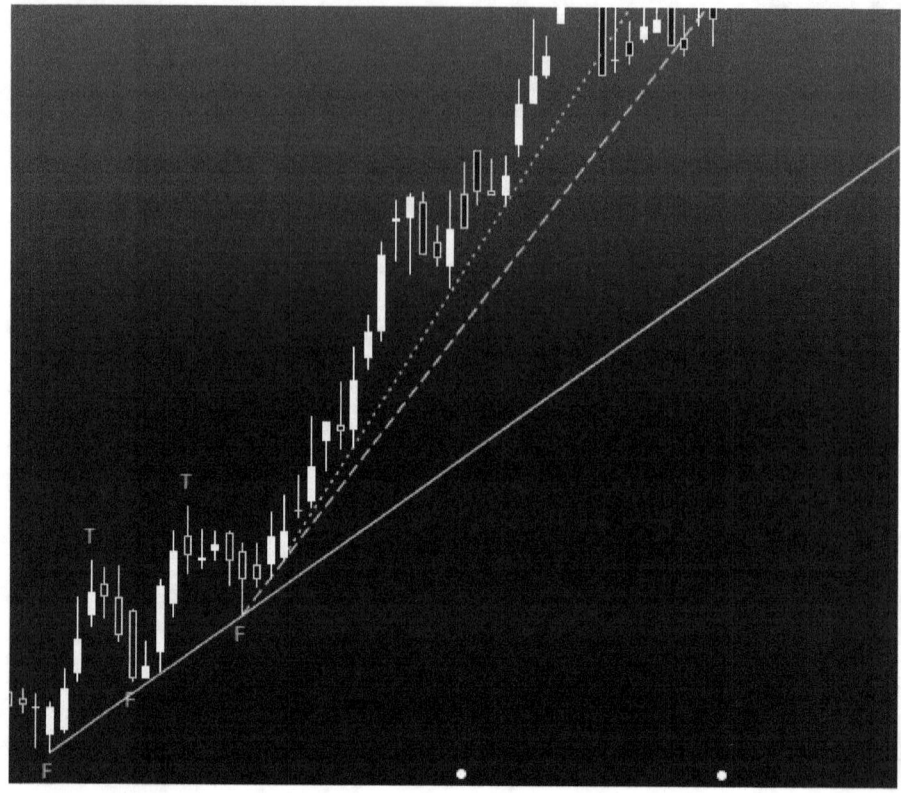

Notice how the tertiary UPTREND LINE is of extreme value to our Scalps in this channel.

While the primary UPTREND LINE only gave 2 touches in that graphic range, the tertiary UPTREND LINE gave 5 touches!

There were five opportunities for you to join the operation.

LOW AND HIGH CHANNEL

We have the formation of a channel when the price touches UPTREND LINE and DOWNTREND LINE, maintaining a decreasing direction.

The operation logic is the same as the rectangle. If a return point occurs near one of the channel boundaries, the assertiveness is greater.

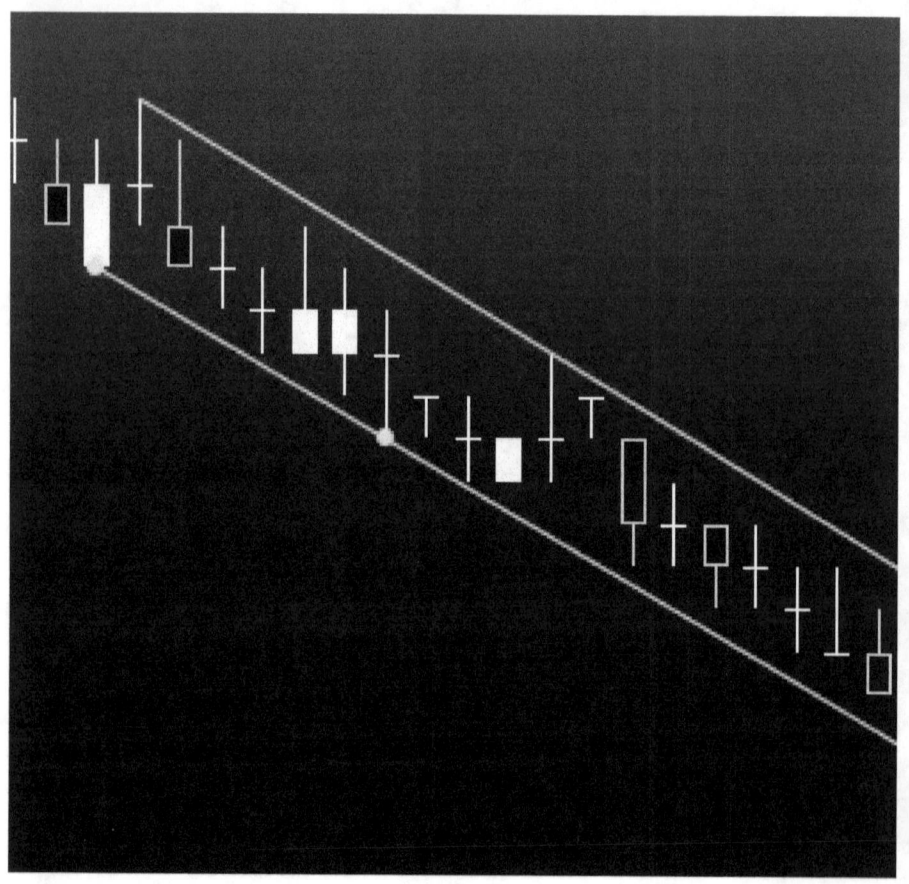

Now, let us see the following image, where the asset was in rectangular consolidation, and then began to make ascending tops and bottoms, inaugurating a high channel.

Notice the candle pointed at the arrow.

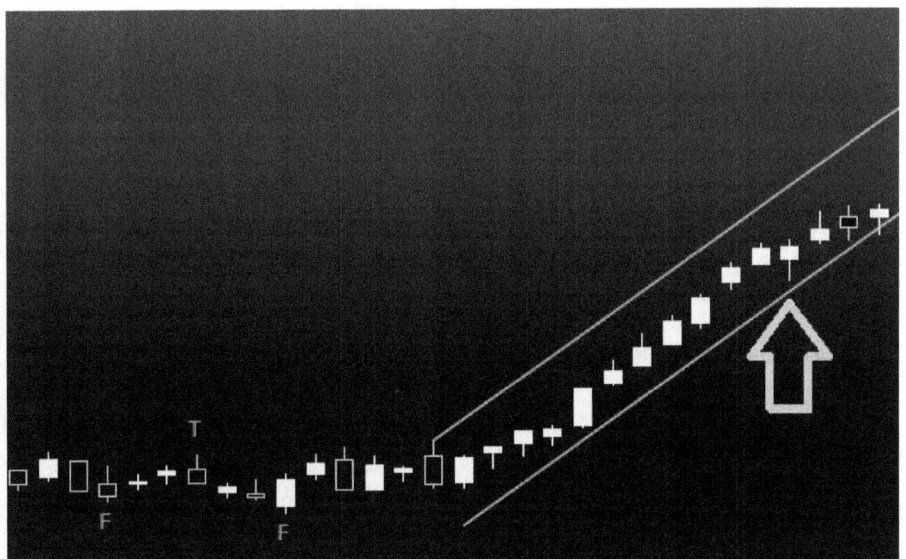

The candle pointed at the arrow was a point where you would be ready to start the operation, even more with the minimum of it besides being smaller than the previous bottom, still beirou the base of the channel.

However, the next candle did not break the slightest. Worse, it made tops and bottoms up, confirming the uptrend.

If you had entered the operation you would have activated the stop loss, because you did not wait for confirmation of the loss of the return candle fund.

MOVING AVERAGES

Moving averages serve to facilitate reading, making it more objective.

They are also useful for you to identify which averages the price is respecting the most, indicating the average that weight traders are using, in addition to being a relevant statistical data.

Media sits as support and resistance, and most Operational Setups (automatic modes and operation objectives) use moving averages.

The averages are so that you can track the market.

If the market is on an uptrend, prices will be above moving averages, driving them up. This also increases the likelihood of formation of ascending tops and bottoms.

If the market is in a downtrend, prices are below moving averages, pushing those averages down. With this, we have a higher chance of occurrence of tops and descending backgrounds.

As we do Scalp, we need to use faster moving averages, and so we use exponential averages, that is, the ones that put greater weight for the latest prices.

The suggestion of use for Scalp is MME 17 (Exponential Moving Average of 17 periods), MME 72 and MME 200.

Let's visualize it on the chart. The exponential average of 17 periods is traced as the continuous line. MME 72 is dashed, while the 200 exponential period is dotted.

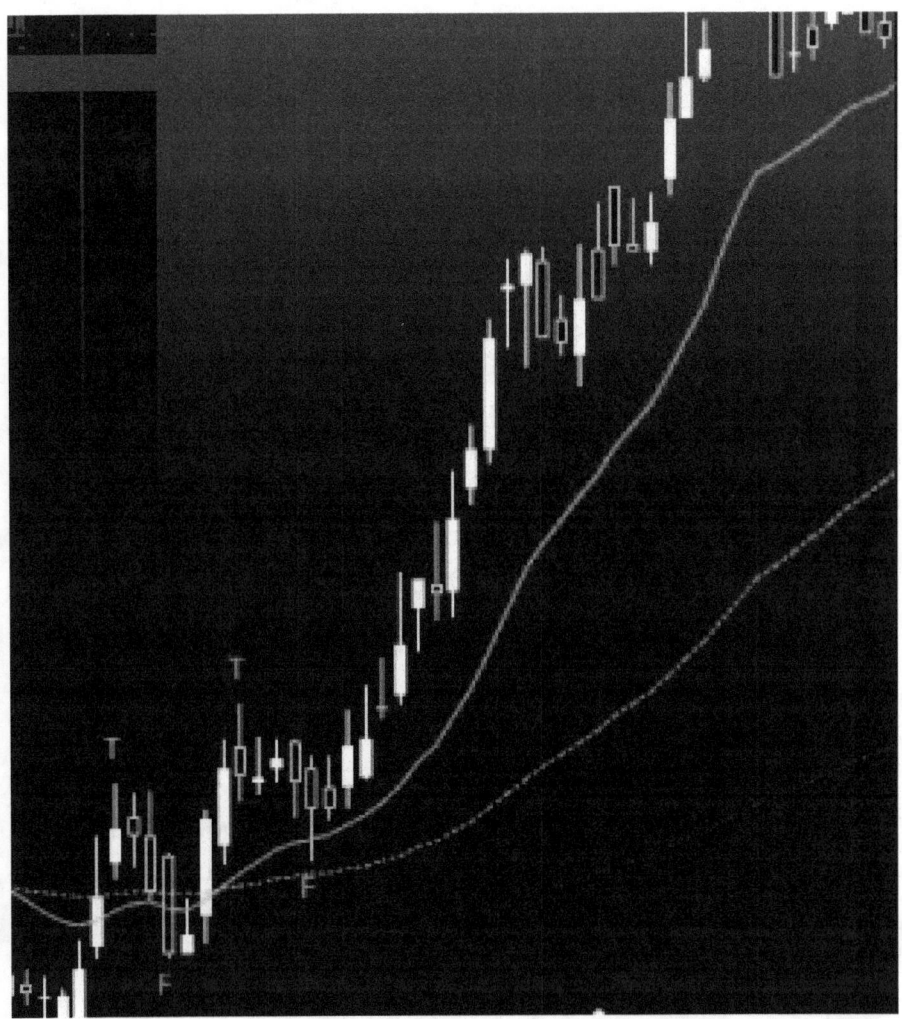

In the above case, if the price breaks the average of 17 periods down, you start using mme 72 as support, which is your next average.

If you break this 72-period, your next purchase will be evaluated as you approach the MME200, which is where you will wait for your return point.

Nothing prevents you from getting sold when you lose any of the averages, as long as there is confirmation of the return point and you have observed in time.

OPERATION OUTPUT - STOP LOSS MOVEMENT

The time to enter operations you already understand.

And after the operation is opened, when should you leave?

That is, where to allocate your Stop Loss?

As already mentioned, every operation needs to be protected in both profit and loss.

No doubt, the best stop loss location is the so-called technical stop, i.e., just below the last fund (if you are going to operate purchased) or just above the last top (if you are going to operate sold)

Let us see in the chart:

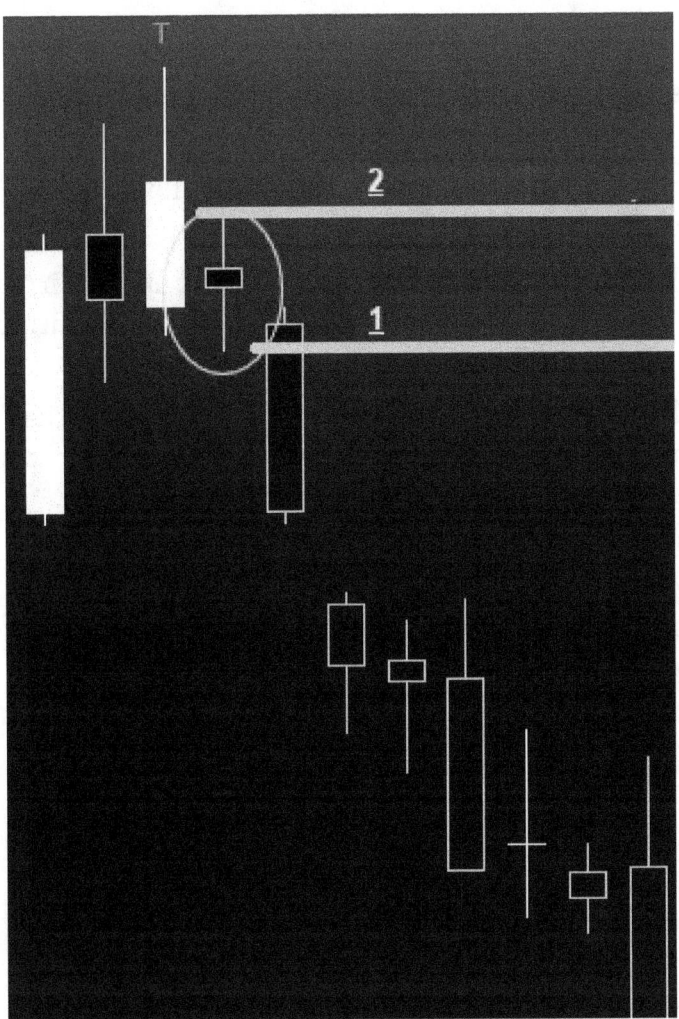

Note that the chart has stopped making tops and bottoms up, generating the candle of doubt we saw in the previous topics. It is the return point circled in yellow.

If on the next candle the price loses the minimum of this return candle, I enter sold in the operation, with my stop there at the maximum of the candle of the return point. The entry of the operation was at point 1.

Remember that you are a Scalper, seek short operations. You should not put too long a stop. Therefore the recommendation is that of the maximum of the candle of doubt. Stop Loss at point 2.

However, if you want a technical-conservative Stop, you can use the last confirmed bottom or top.

The confirmation of the top or bottom is the same as the trend confirmation.

Remember that we say that the uptrend is only confirmed when the last top is broke, and the downtrend is only confirmed when the last fund is broke.

When there is the breakout of the last top, we say that the last fund has been confirmed, and then you can put your stop at this point because the uptrend has been confirmed.

In the next top confirmation, you will have the opportunity to "raise" your stop to the next bottom, and then your stop loss becomes stop gain, in addition to your stop of the target which is also gain.

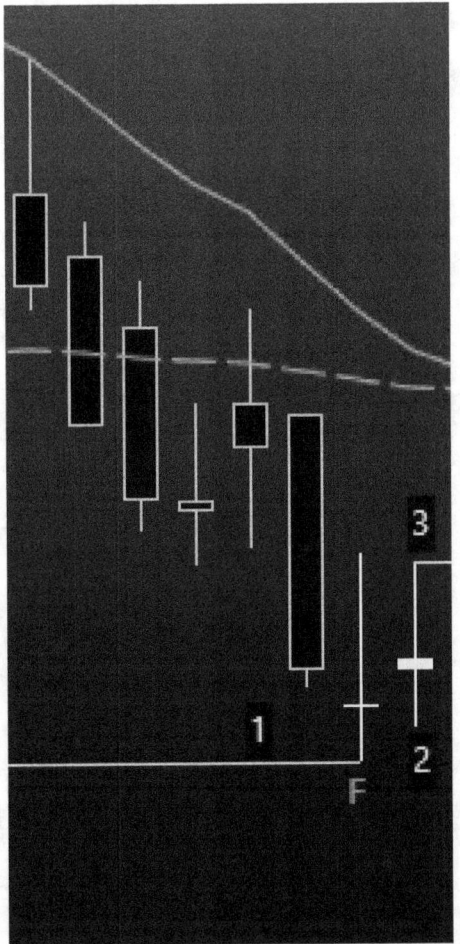

On the arrow pointed at 2 we have the candle of doubt. There the chart did not generate a new fund and aroused scalper's attention. He has already set his entry in the top break marked at 3 on the chart.

There on line 1 is the initial Stop Loss position. You will raise this stop as the trade evolves.

Then, after the next top, your stop will go up. Let us see the progression of the trade:

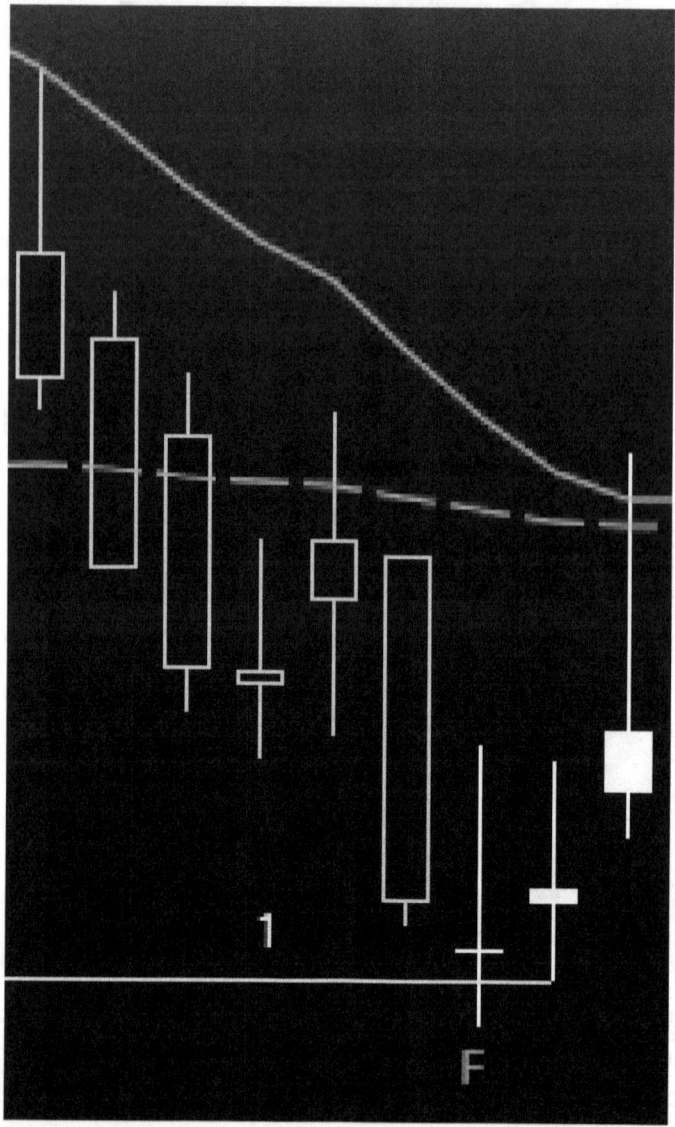

Now we move the stop loss (point 1 on the chart) to the minimum of the candle before the current one.

We see that this was possible because the candle made top and bottom up, indicating the ascent. Let's see the sequence.

TRAINING FOR SCALPER

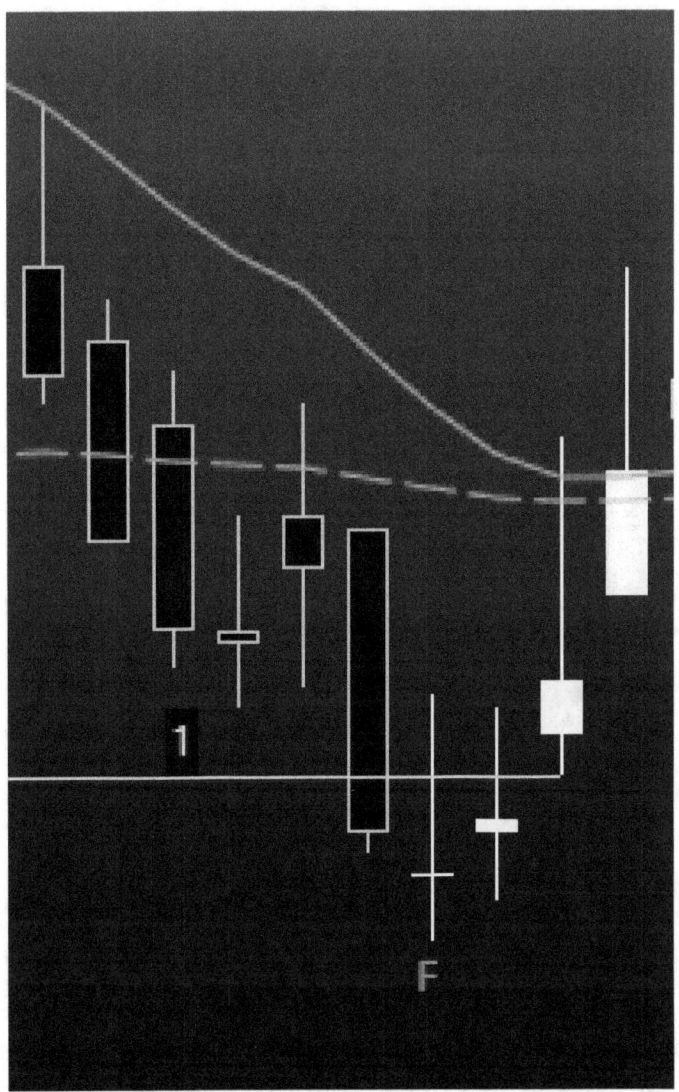

The trade has evolved well. Again a candle of tops and upper bottoms. This allows us to place the stop loss higher up at the last bottom (minimum of the previous candle).

That is, while the asset is making upstream funds, I am in the trade.

Let us see what happened next.

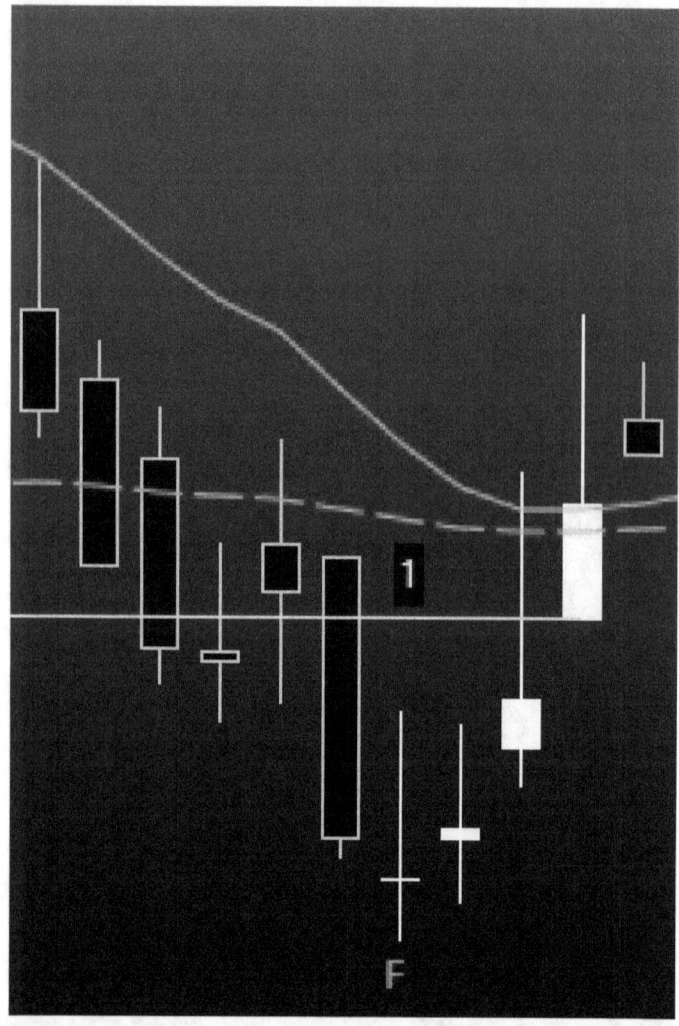

We once again observe an upward background, allowing us to raise the stop to point 1 of the chart, that is, the last bottom. But that's WRONG. And why is it wrong to raise this stop right now?

Simple. The current candle did not make a bigger top. She didn't confirm the trend. So we can be close to a retraction or a trend change. (it is a point of attention!).

The most appropriate thing to do is to perform the operation at least partially. 50% achievement.

And keep the Stop in the position of the previous image, and not elevate it as we did in this image above.

TIME CHARTS

As already mentioned, Scalper must operate in more than one time period.

But which one should I choose to be the largest chart, and which one will be the smallest?

Your anchor chart, reference, guide, should be the largest chart, and it can be the 15-minute, 60-minute, daily, weekly, and even monthly chart.

The fine-tuning chart varies from the 1-minute chart to the daily chart.

But you cannot reference the daily chart and fine-tune it at 1 minute. There is no point in that.

Below I present table with the correlation indicated:

Base Graphic	Month	Week	Day	60 minutes	15 minutes
Deep Graphic	Day	60 minutes	15 minutes	5 minutes	1 minute

That is, if you use the Daily chart as an anchor, you must then use the 15-minute chart to perform the entry in the operation.

You will mark brackets, resistances, UPTREND LINE, DOWNTREND LINE, in the journal. And then go to the 15-minute chart in order to increase the assertiveness of operations.

Possibly operate with the daily chart and the 15-minute chart or with the 60-minute chart and the 5-minute chart is the lowest level for a human to perform on scalping.

Using the 1-minute chart is possible, but it generates a lot of noise, and the hit index of operations drops dramatically.

THE USE OF FIBONACCI

In Scalping you use the Fibonacci Retraction and Projection tool in the same way that you use it in other operations with graphical analysis.

The projections that really matter are 161.8% and 100%. These are the targets you are going to plot.

In the field of entry of the operation, the Retraction tool will have as main uses the levels of 38.2%, 50% and 61.8% of Fibonacci.

That is, the entry of the operation is more assertive if it is between 38.2% and 50% Fibonacci.

> *You can only use the Fibonacci retraction tool if the previous background is confirmed.*

The above statement is particularly important. It is not appropriate to try to predict the end of a retraction using Fibonacci if you still do not know if it will be a retraction or a trend change.

Therefore, you can only predict the size of the retraction using Fibonacci after the price breaks the last top, because there will be confirmed the bottom.

TRAINING FOR SCALPER

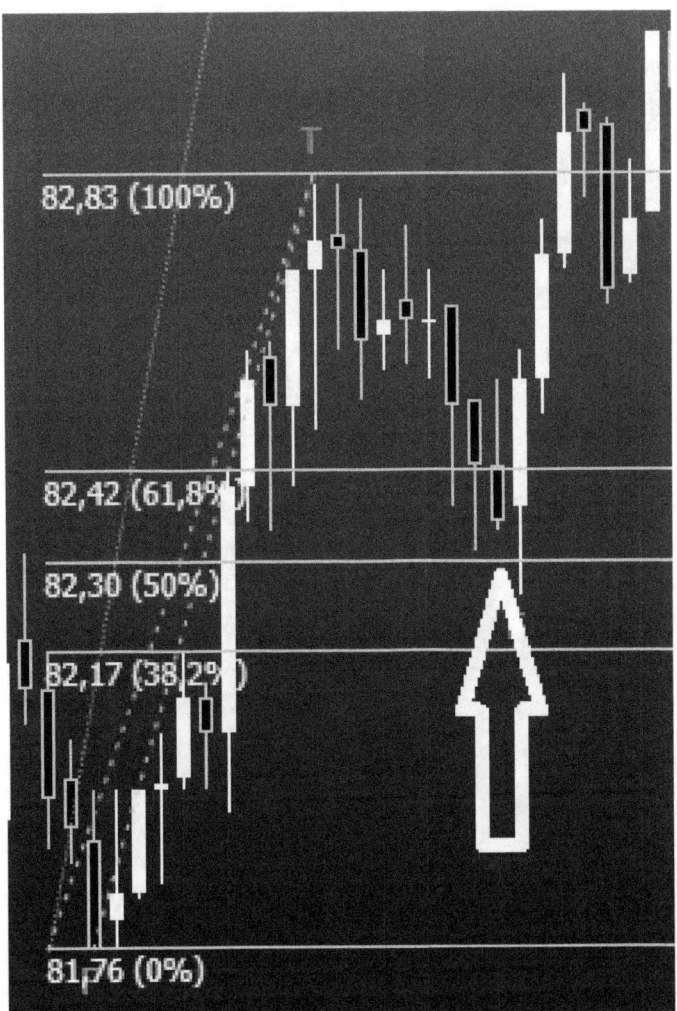

In the picture we see that there was a price downturn at the level 50%.

Also, note that a return point pointed by the arrow was generated, as the candle did not make a lower bottom and still made a higher top.

Then, there was the disruption of the maximum of this return candle, generating opportunity for increased position or even entry into the operation by retraction.

Right. I got into the operation. And now, what is my target?

To do this, you will use Fibonacci projection:

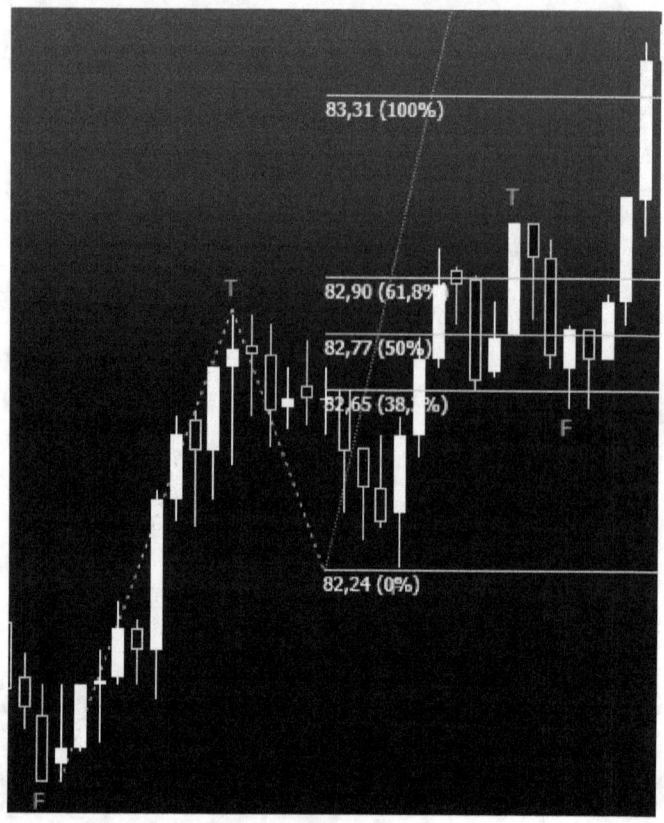

This trade would have generated success and you would have reached the 100% Fibonacci point.

At that point, you would make a partial realization of 50% of your position, and you would remain in the stop loss operation always positioned at the last bottom.

The sequence would be as follows:

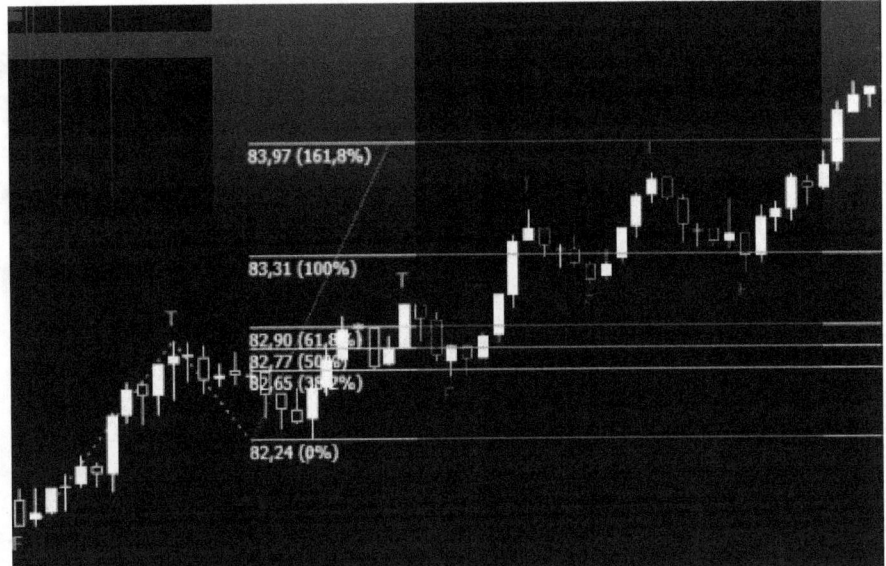

That is, you would reach the level 161.8% fibonacci, performing the remaining 50% and finally ending the operation in full success.

GRAPHIC PATTERNS

The graphic patterns are figures that we observe in the sets of candles in order to foresee some market situation.

The patterns are to predict 3 situations:

The first situation is the resumption of the trend. It happens when the market is sideways and then a breakout occurs, as in the channel, returning to the previous trend.

The second is the continuity of the trend. It's the best standard. The market is directional and only performs a brief retraction to continue in the trend. The flag is an example of a graphic figure that identifies continuity.

Finally, we have the situation of trend reversal. In this situation the role is rising, makes a slight retraction as in continuity and when it reaches again the previous top he can not overcome it. It is a great entry with short stop to enter sold (stop above the top that has not been overcome).

Now let us evaluate the patterns and see what is the most likely of the above 3 situations for each of them.

HIGH FLAG

The flag is a high reliability standard.

It indicates a great possibility of resuming the trend after this slight pause in the climb that characterizes the high flag. Look at the picture.

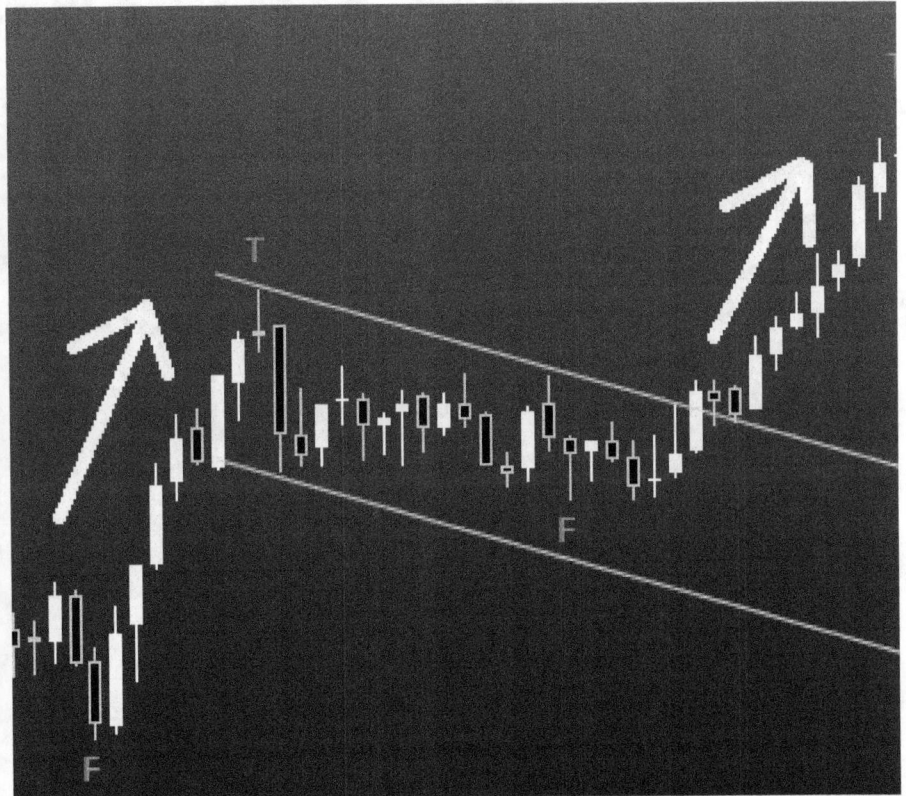

The flag is this downchannel within the uptrend. Notice that the price gets stuck in the channel, slowly goes down without losing the previous background. And all of a sudden, he breaks through the channel and continues the upward trend.

To set up the flag are required at least 2 candles.

See how the candle that breaks the channel inaugurated the return of the uptrend.

And where would the entrance be and where would the stop be? In the following image, the entry takes place at point 1, that is, in the channel break. while the stop should be positioned at the bottom of the channel at point 2.

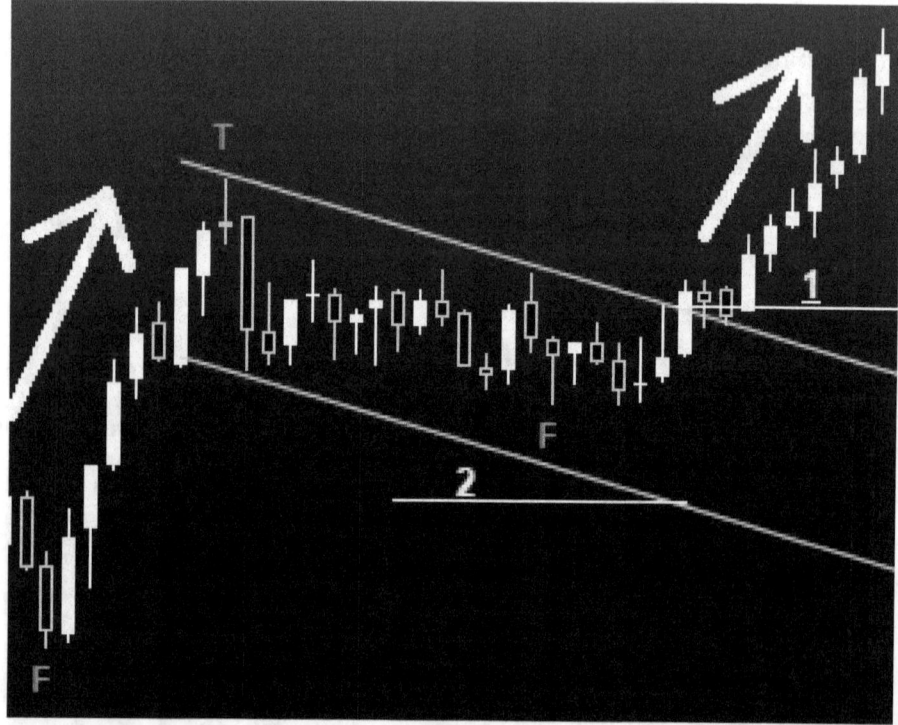

To calculate the target of the operation, that is, the maximum profit point where you have already performed and ended the operation, we will see the following image where straight 1 indicates the mast of that flag.

You will project this mast from the breakup. It will replicate the mast at the breakpoint upwards, as we see in straight 2. At the top of bar 2 you will position your maximum stop gain. But as we have already said, you can and should partially realize your profits after price advances and raising your stop.

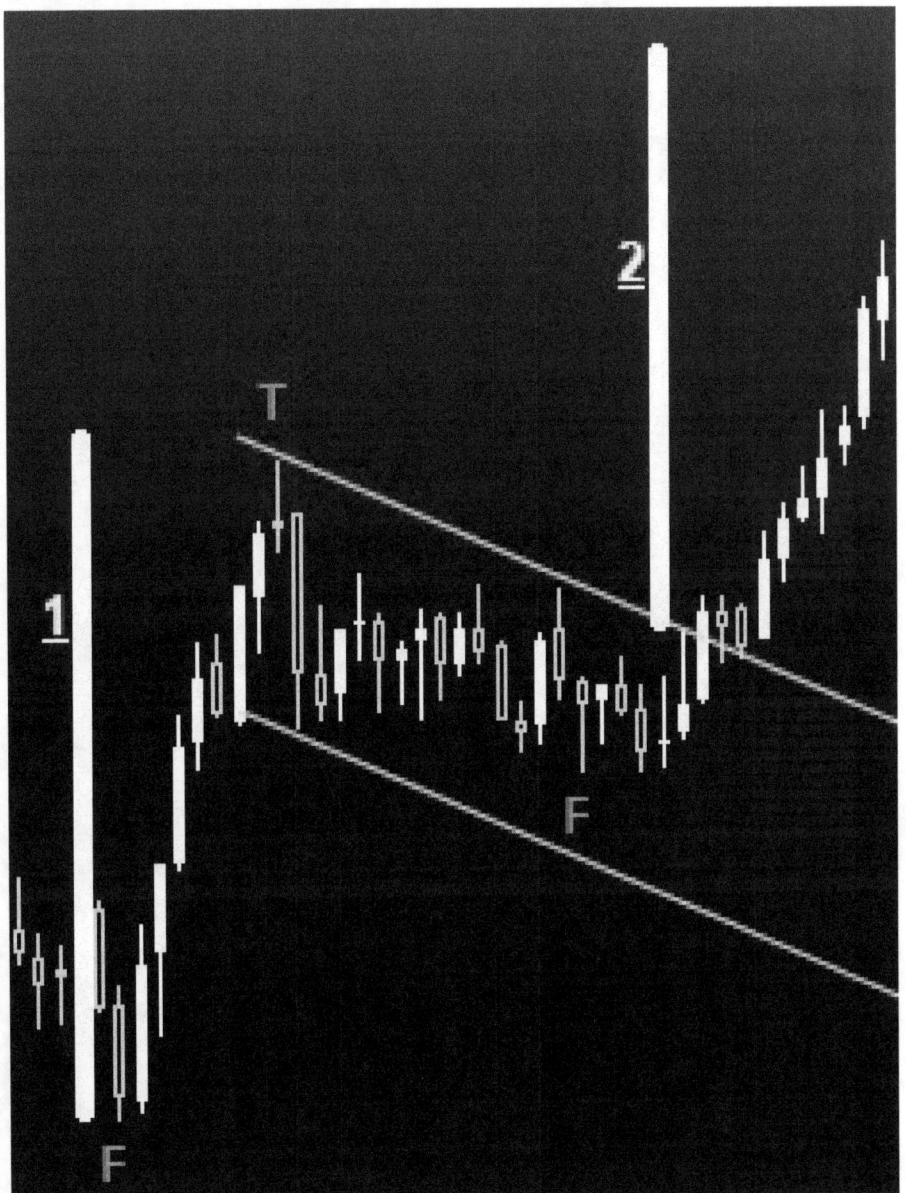

Flags usually appear after a strong high cycle. Usually the trend is so strong that it does not even reach 50% fibonacci. And then to enter the operation the ideal is to operate the high flag. And usually, these flags occur twice in a row, increasing the chance of entry.

LOW FLAG

Similarly, in a downtrend, it is possible that after a strong movement the asset will make a slight retraction in channel without reaching the level 50% fibonacci and then return to its downtrend.

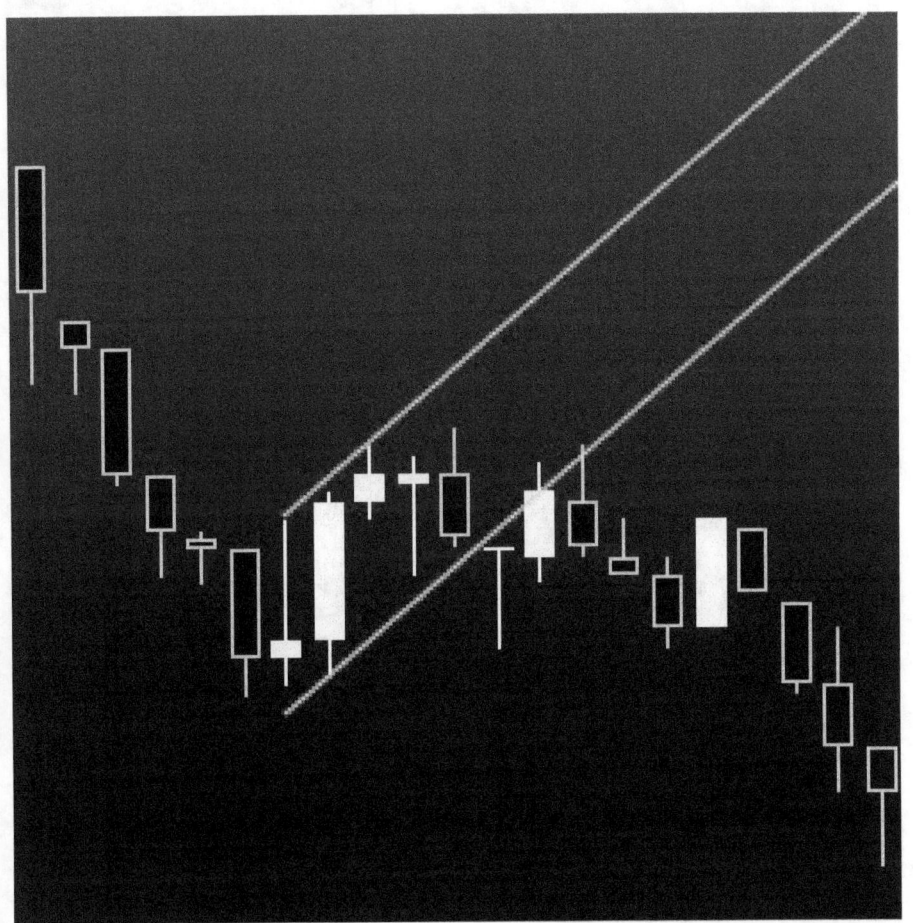

In this situation, our entry will be in the disruption of the channel, where we will enter sold, positioning our stop loss at the upper limit of the channel at the time of entry.

We do it because it is a channel. That's always the channel stop. If the breakout is false, it will not trigger the stop loss. It will only slow down the operation because the asset will remain in the channel.

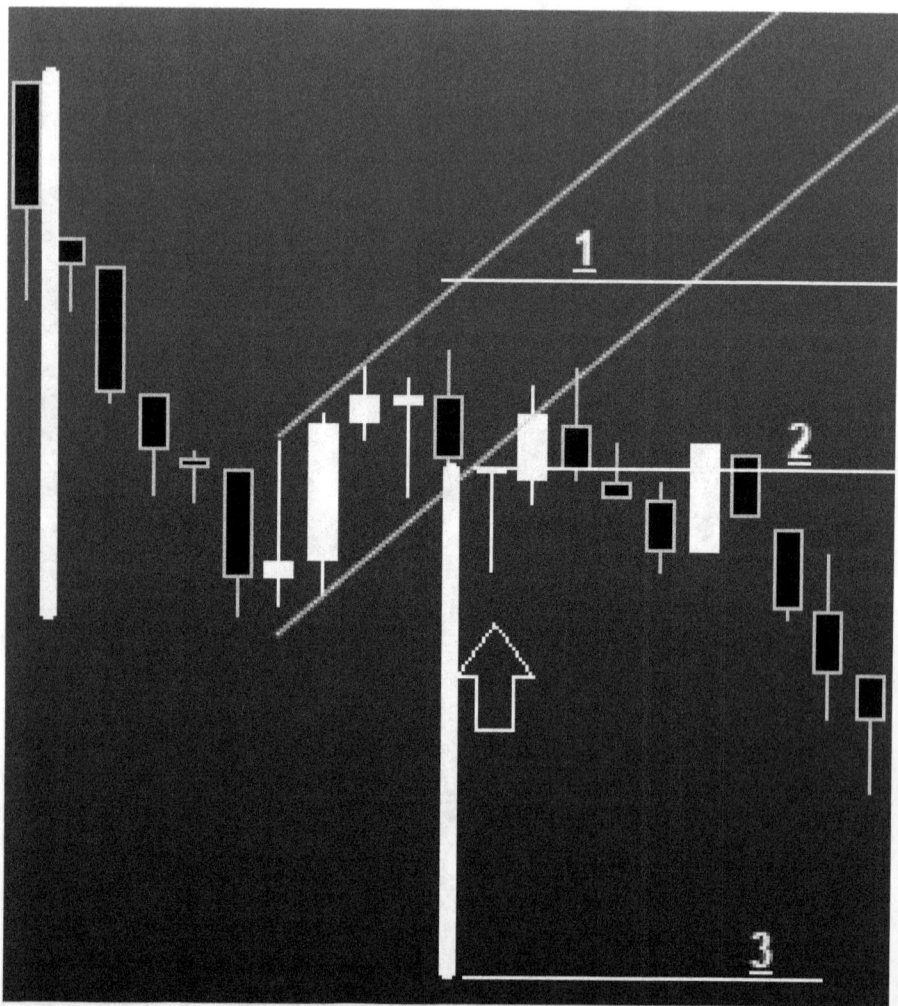

Therefore, on straight 1 we position our stop loss, with operation entry in 2 there in the channel break down, as indicated in the arrow. (the candle closed below the channel).

Similarly, we must project the mast down to position our stop gain as in straight 3 of the images.

FLAG AFTER CONSOLIDATION CHANNEL

Flags that occur after a consolidation channel are usually more effective and have stronger movements.

For example, imagine that the market spent a lot of time there varying in the same price range.

Suddenly, it sticks the channel down and starts the downtrend. Then makes a light flag. You prepare your entrance and enter the channel disruption.

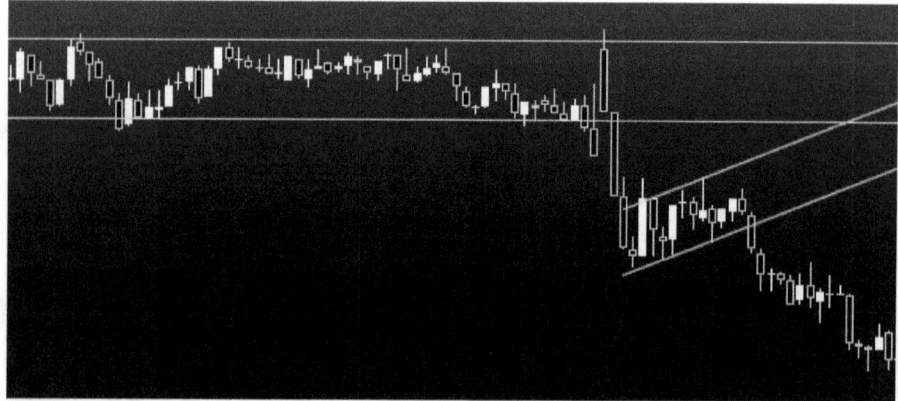

Notice that in the image above you would end up having your stop loss activated because you would enter the operation on the candle that pierced the channel down, but the asset gave a "violinada" up and then made the sudden movement down. You would have the stop activated above the channel!

This was because the channel in the image above was not marked correctly on the chart. Candles have been purposely omitted so you don't make that mistake. See the full picture of the chart, with some candles on the left.

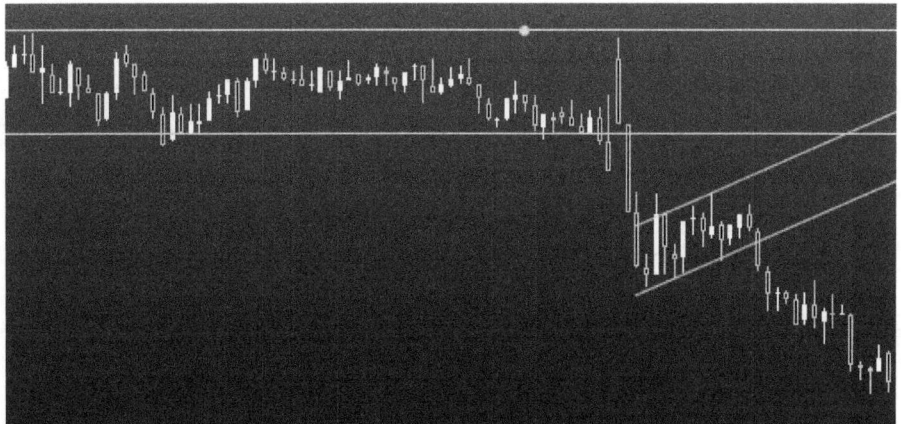

This was to show you that the lack of attention when delimiting the channel can cost you the entire operation and the loss of a beautiful entry.

But why not operate the channel? Why not keep buying at the base of the canal and selling the canal ceiling? Why, scalper doesn't operate without a trend! The operation of buying and selling the channel is complex, gives a lot of work, is risky because it can be easily violined at its stop, and the worst, presents little gain.

OPERATION IN AVERAGE DISRUPTION

For this strategy, we use more than one time chart.

The idea is to locate points where the chart is touching without breaking, and that these points are in more than one time chart and in more than one candle.

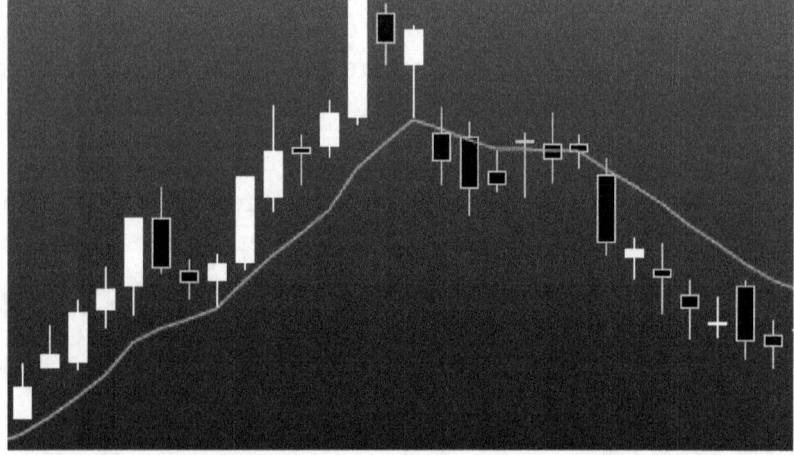

Notice how the asset had been respecting the exponential moving average of 9 periods, always remaining above it and in an uptrend.

By breaking the average down, he did not sustain himself and reversed the downward trend, initiating the reverse movement.

Notice that there is a return point on this chart at the top of the movement. The next candle, low, did not make a new top and a new bottom. You would enter the breakout and your stop loss would be at the maximum of the return candle, which has not been activated and you would make a nice trade down.

But here we are talking about the disruption of the exponential moving average of 9 periods. The reversal of this trend was already announced by the point of return, but even if you had not realized, you would enter "late" in the operation, but would earn money.

ALIGNMENT OF TIME CHARTS

As already said, the ideal is that any signal appears in more than one time chart at the same time. This powers the signal.

Let us take as an example the daily chart of an asset. Notice that it came in downtrend, formed the low flag (slight channel up), and then hitched again the strong descent.

In addition, there was also the presence of a double top, the violation down the moving average that guided it and the point of attention with the low sail at the top of the flag. Let's look at this daily chart.

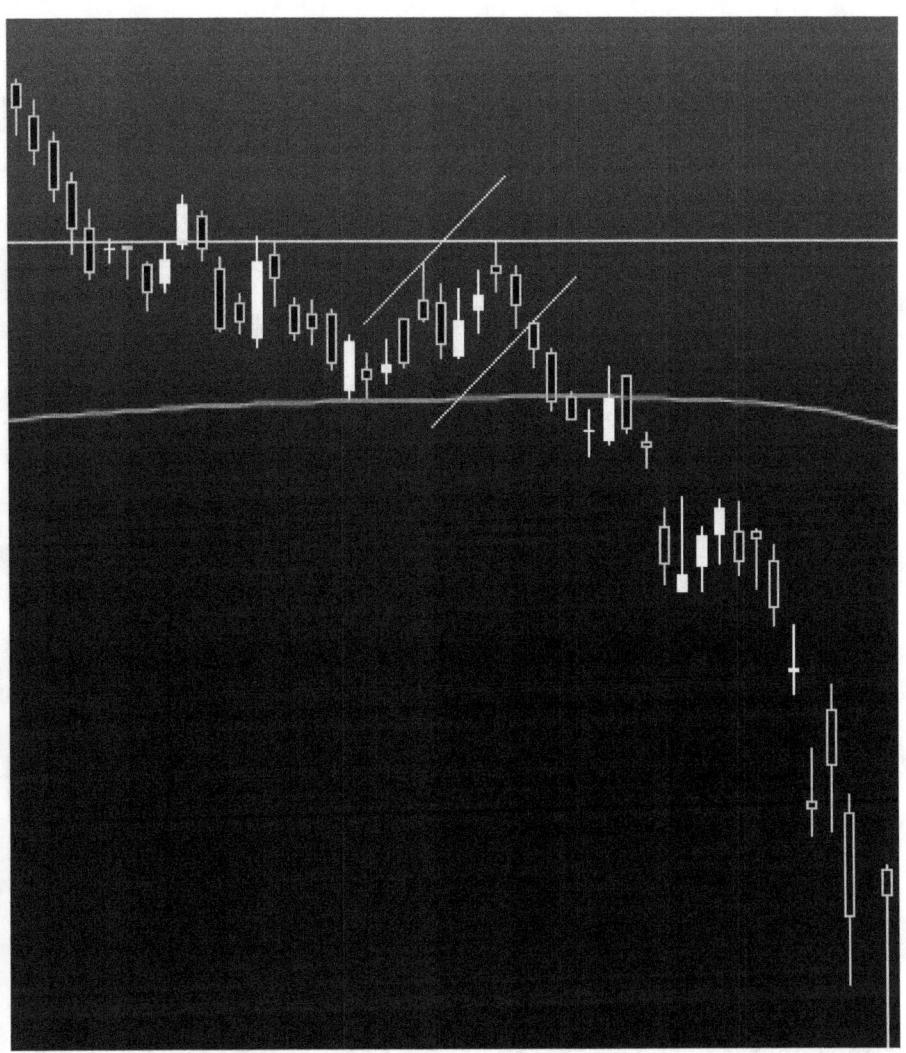

Soon, you evaluated the daily chart, noticed the flag, watched the double top, and migrated to the 15-minute chart to adjust your entry into the operation.

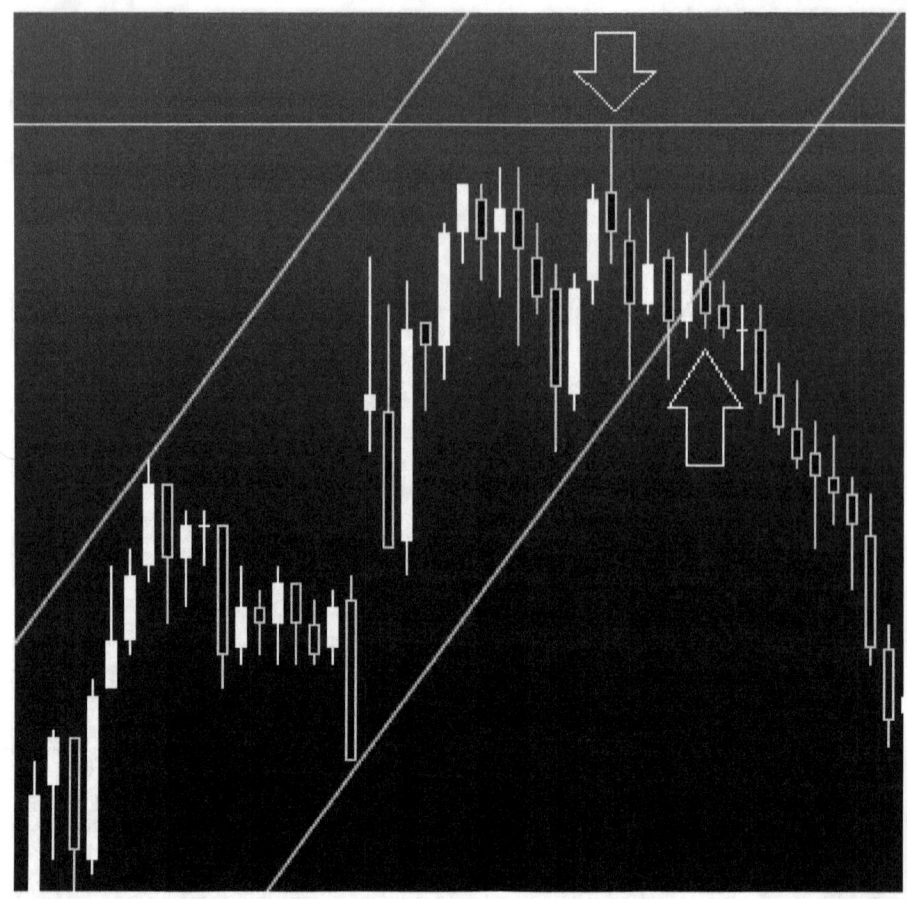

In the 15-minute chart the situation was confirmed. There occurred the touch at the top without confirming breakout, characterizing the double top at least momentarily, and at the same time generated the attention candle because it became negative, indicating that the sellers won in the last 15 minutes in this attention candle.

From there you could enter if you wanted to but if you are even more careful you will wait for the breakup of the low flag, and that is what occurred right after, generating your entry.

Unbelievably valuable is the situation in which we find a pivot in the larger chart and this also reproduces in the smaller chart.

As the pattern was predicted in the daily chart, this operation could even become a sold Swing Trade if the Scalper feels free to do so.

Remember, no one should be a pure Scalper. The secret is to diversify! Balance!

FIBONACCI CORRECTION ENTRY

Here the Scalper will operate only with the 1-minute chart and using the 15-minute time as a macro reference.

You will seek entry at the point of return, and will focus on the retractions of Fibonacci, more precisely between level 61.8% and 38.2%, with special attention in the proximity of the level 50%.

Your goal is to get to the end of a slight retraction of a trend.

You will plot Fibonacci retraction starting at the previous bottom and ending at the top where the retraction began.

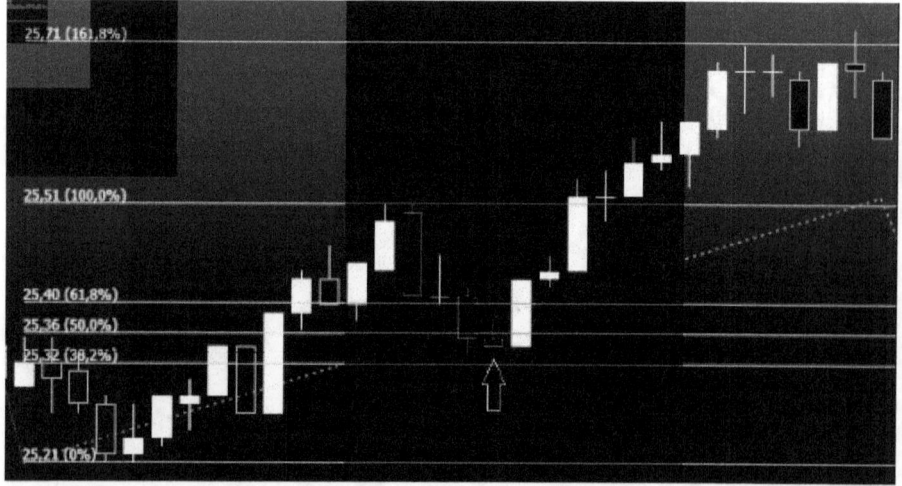

See the return point marked on the arrow, at the end of the retraction and close to the level 50% of Fibonacci.

There is your entrance. Stop Loss there at the minimum of the previous candle (or return if the previous candle is too expensive).

To calculate the gain, you must use the other tool called Fibonacci Projection.

The projection will trace you from the bottom to the top before the retraction, and then finish it at the bottom of the retraction, giving you levels of 100% and 161.8% that will be your partial and final gains, respectively.

Let us see what the operation would look like.

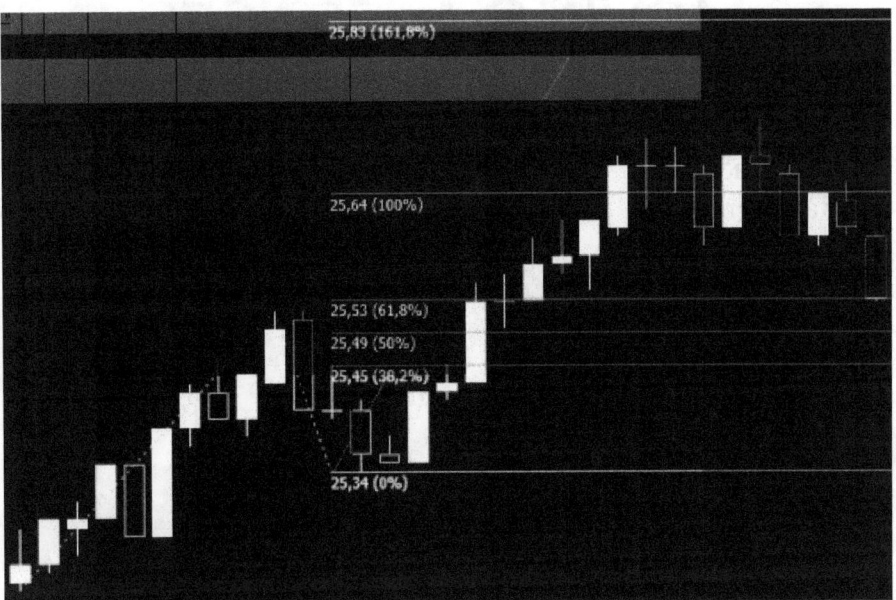

In this operation you would perform the partial gain at 100% Fibonacci, and would be towed then performing fully at the same level. In this case it did not reach 161.8% but ended with profit.

ENTRY TO CORRECTION BY MOVING AVERAGES

We should also be aware of corrections that touch the moving average, and especially when the moving average is broken up after a downtrend.

Soon after there will be a retraction that will touch that medium, to test it. If you form a return point there, your input is configured.

Let us see in the picture how it would look.

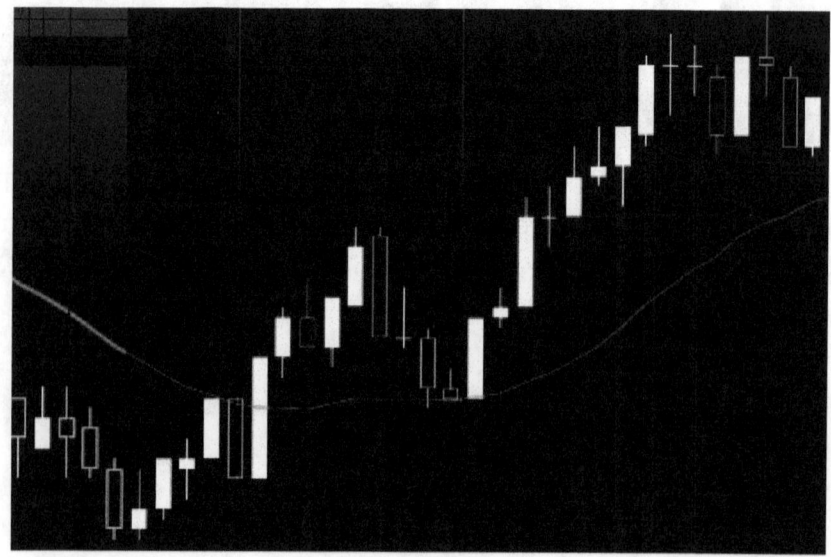

You will open the buy operation on the basis of this return point as we have already explained, but your gain may be either by Fibonacci, or in the next breakup of the moving average down, when it will possibly end the uptrend that has arisen.

The most recommended is to use Fibonacci at least for partial achievement in 100%.

ENTRY IN TRENDLINE CORRECTION

Another way to operate retractions is through trend lines. Let us demonstrate visually.

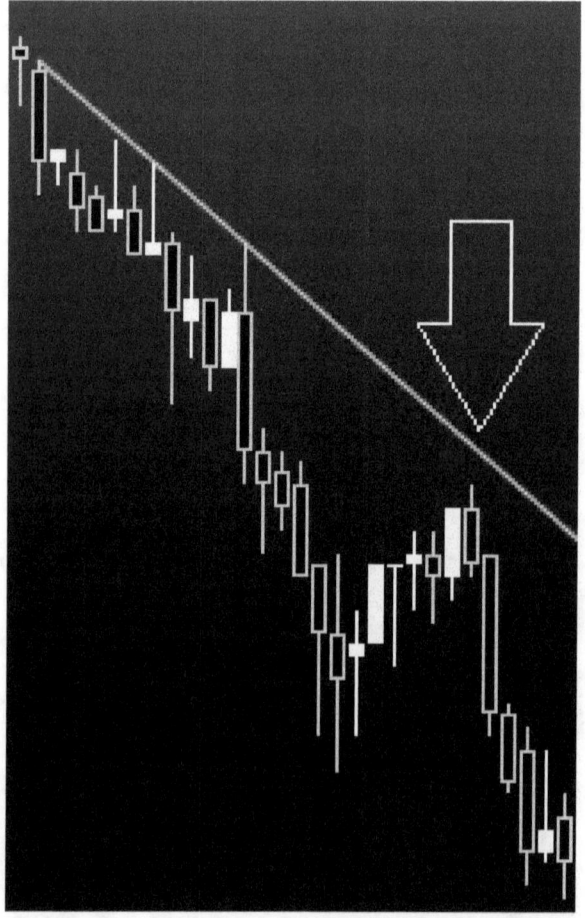

In the image we can see the downtrend line. The asset then goes into slight retraction and then approaches the DOWNTREND LINE that already had 4 touches, that is, a considerable resistance.

The asset did not have the strength to break the DOWNTREND LINE and then resumed its downtrend.

Note that in this case there was no time for the attention candle. The return candle was a low marobozu (large sail). So Scalper would only enter that trade if he operated the flag that formed there. Because in the breaking of the flag this operation would be assertive.

DOUBLE TOPS AND DOUBLE BOTTOMS

The double-top and double-bottom graphic figures are especially important not only for the scalper but also for any speculator.

The reason for this is the huge amount of Stop Loss that will be positioned there at that point, given that operators expect it not to lose the bottom or not win the top.

It is a very explosive moment. This is what always generates a marobozu (huge candle) after the expiration of any resistance.

Let us see the picture:

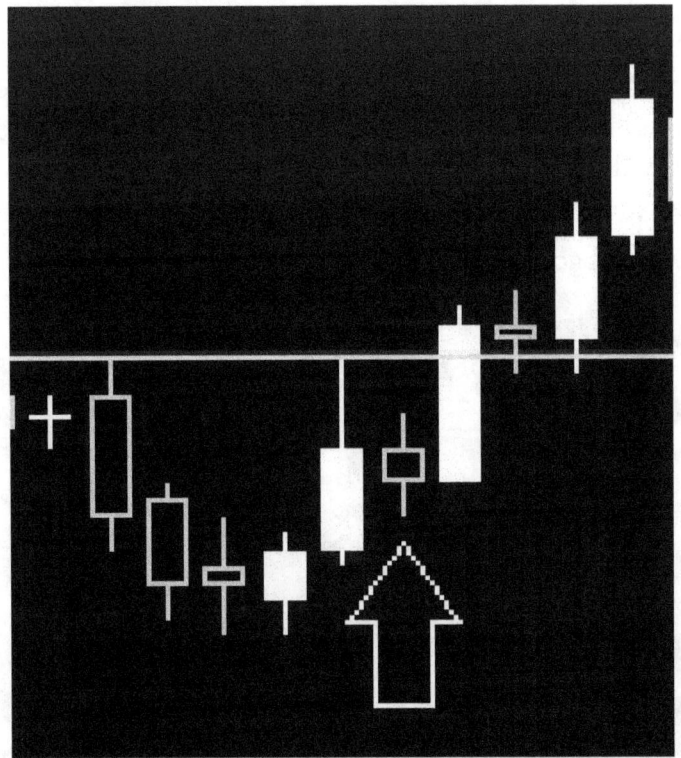

There above the double top line is a large amount of stop loss of those who are operating sold, and the stop gain of those who are bought. You as a scalper are keeping an eye on these stops.

The candle pointed at the arrow needs to be a slight retraction. The next candle will go to the top and you will enter this breakup, to catch the stop of the sold. Your stop loss will be positioned at the minimum of the candle pointed at the arrow. If it falls below it, it probably reverses the trend and no longer surpasses the top.

For assertiveness in the breakage of the double top, the second candle that tested this top ideally must be positive, and in the case of the double bottom, the second candle that tested the bottom preferably needs to be negative.

If it is not a positive candle testing the double top, unless this second candle is not a trend reversal candle pattern. Same for the bottom. It cannot be a reversal pattern.

If it is some pattern and the candle is still opposed to the movement, it is highly likely that the double top is not overcome, because if the second candle is negative, the sellers are already winning!

Here is what is going to happen.

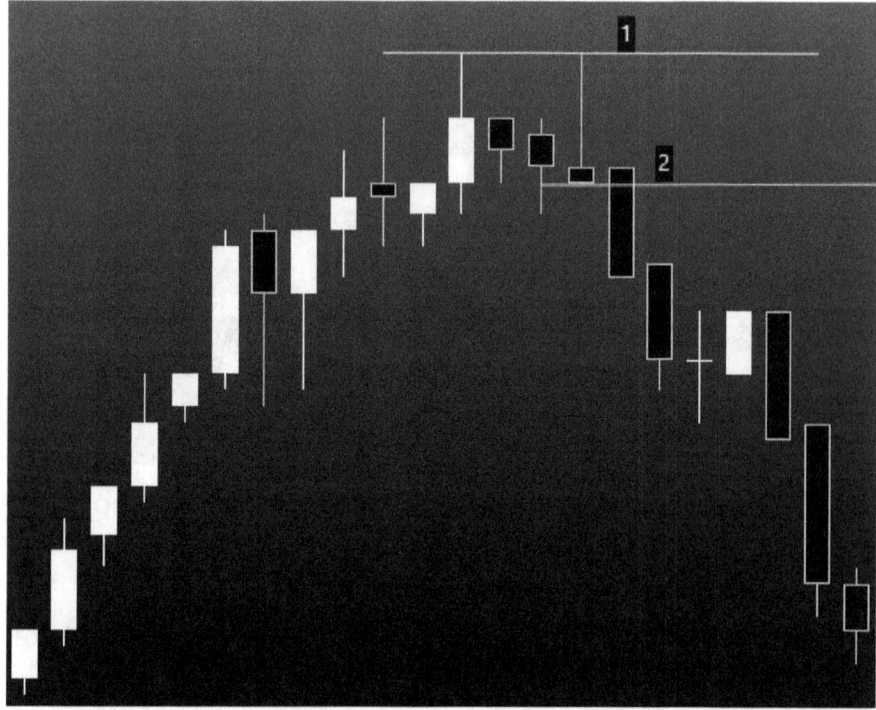

In the illustrative image, in addition to the second candle that tested the top being negative, an inverted hammer was formed, putting even more pressure so that the top is not broken.

Point 2 is where the entry of the operation will be positioned, that is, right after the candle that generated the double top. Your stop loss will be at the maximum of this candle at point 1. That is, you do not operate breakup here. Just see the candle from the second top. Of course, the sellers are strong!

The double top and double bottom are priceless. You can make money either by breaking from the top or bottom, and in the test that does not surpass you.

CONGESTION DISRUPTION

If a top and a double bottom generate a placement of multiple stop loss in the same location, this happens even more in a congestion.

The longer the congestion, the more explosive the movement of her rupture will be.

There will be a sudden movement, because once activated, the stop loss acts as a buying aggression (in the case of those sold) or a sales aggression (in the case of those purchased).

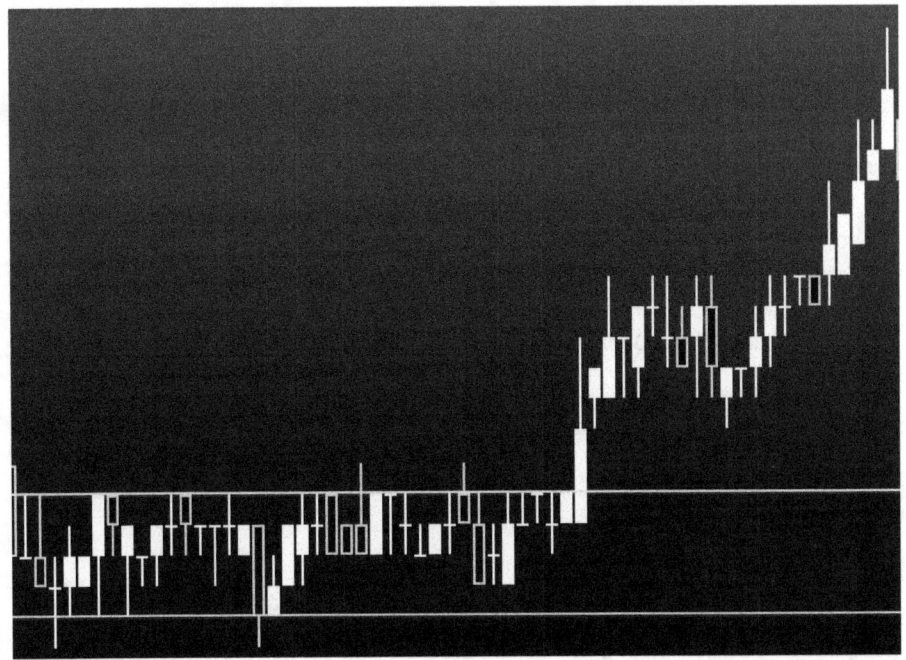

Notice how the asset was oscillating in the congestion range, and then in the first breakup there was the explosion.

In the same candle of the explosion there is a wick above, indicating that some speculators have already made profits there, possibly because they projected the partial target replicating up the height of the congestion channel.

SCALPER X ROBOTS

You as Scalper also can not look only at tops and bottoms, volumes, etc.

> Do this mental exercise: If it were automatic like this, robots would be cash machines. There's always human analysis behind it. Scalper is not purely mathematical. You would be defeated by the machine!

To beat a robot, you need to use intuition, emotional of other players, because these characteristics are the ones that differentiate your brain from a robot.

And the worst. Robots are set up to fool you!

Although such a practice is prohibited, it is highly common for you to view on any trading floor and any active a large player robot positioning huge orders to attract the market and then withdraws the order and reverses aside as soon as the asset reaches the price it desired.

Those who operate options are already used to seeing robots duelling all day in a certain derivative without even an order being executed! Robots change the value of the option only by mathematically calculating according to the movement of the asset price.

So, do not even try to duel mathematically with a robot because you will be defeated.

You need to operate with the sentimentality of the other players in the market.

The robot only increases the force of movement. It is human

beings who initiate the movement!

This is because the machine does not take the initiative. It only manages after the human has already altered the environment around him.

Remember that.

CONCLUSION

We thus finalize its preparation to perform short and fast operations in the market based on objective criteria of action.

Subjectivity, that is, the touch of intuition and emotion, is the responsibility of the scalper, who must always measurement it based on the thinking of the other speculators and not on himself.

This analysis is useful when you are in doubt whether or not you enter an operation that is already fully positioned. But never to go into an operation that does not have the signs we saw in this book.

And most importantly, put in your mind that you should diversify your investments.

You must have fixed income money, you must have money in dividend stocks, you must conduct short-term trades, and you must carry scalps when the signals arise.

That is how someone in charge puts the money to work.

BOOKS BY THIS AUTHOR

Operating On The Stock Exchange In 5 Days

For Begginers

www.ingramcontent.com/pod-product-compliance
Lightning Source LLC
Chambersburg PA
CBHW050248220526
45465CB00002B/590